PASSIVE
SOLAR HOUSE
BASICS

PASSIVE SOLAR HOUSE BASICS

Peter van Dresser

Previously Published as Homegrown Sundwellings

ANCIENT CITY PRESS
SANTA FE, NEW MEXICO

Printed and bound in the United States of America
on acid-free paper.

Cover illustration and design by Faith deLong

First Ancient City Press edition

Van Dresser, Peter.
    [Homegrown sundwellings]
    Passive solar house basics / Peter van Dresser.
        p.   cm.
    Originally published: Homegrown sundwellings. Santa Fe, N.M. :
Lightning Tree, 1977.
    Includes bibliographical references (p.   ) and index.
    ISBN 0-941270-90-4 (alk. paper : pbk.)
    1. Solar houses—Design and construction.   I. Title.
TH7413.V36   1996
690'.8370472—dc20   95-37695
                                                                CIP

10 9 8 7 6 5 4 3 2 1

To Florence

Other Books
on Home Construction

The Adobe Book, by John O'Connor. A fully illustrated, detailed how-to book covering every phase of construction. Includes ideas for floor plans, fireplaces and Southwest details.

La Casa Adobe, by William Lumpkins. Elevations and basic floor plans for adobe homes based on historic Southwest houses. Four solar adobe house plans are also on historic Southwest houses. Four solar adobe house plans are also included.

CONTENTS

Figures

Foreword

The recent flood of books and articles on solar energy for buildings has been paralleled by a swelling interest in the owner-built home. These two themes are uniquely fused in *Passive Solar House Basics*—an everyman's guide that could easily become a textbook for the beginning professional in the arts and sciences of buildings. It is intended as a handbook in simple language for the intelligent homeowner—and we are all homeowners to the extent that we control the form and operation of our own dwellings. But we must examine our intelligence when looking at our own all too often frail homes and the kind of consumptive buildings so often recommended by the bounty of our energy-intensive industrialization.

The concept of Homegrown Sundwellings is not an idle theory but an extension of existing and thriving practices. The concept is firmly rooted in the living construction traditions as well as the socioeconomic circumstances of a natural ecological region— the uplands of northern New Mexico. But by being so pertinent to the particulars of a unique place it reveals principles of universal applicability. Although the *intention* of the Sundwellings program is to "strengthen a grassroots movement in New Mexico towards self-help solutions," it becomes a demonstration of both concept and process in developing a mature house culture anywhere.

The universality of the Sundwellings concept is implicit in its two ingredients. *Adobe* has been the universal building tradition of every great early civilization and continues to be the substance of the man-made environment throughout most of the arid and semi-arid world. And the thermal principles of adobe can be transposed to its more complex masonry cousins—the brick or cut stone of many regional traditions, or the poured concrete or unit masonry of industrialized building. The other ingredient, the energy of the *Sun,* is the constant of our earthly existence. It is the only universal energy source. It is also the ultimate renewable energy source.

The popularity of solar energy, especially as a domestic idea, must inevitably encourage the reconsideration of the form and material of the house. Both the mammoth solar research contracts financed in the millions by federal agencies and the back-of-the-envelope studies by one-man contractors come to the same conclusion—that solar energy hardware makes little sense either thermally or economically on a poorly designed building or when not closely tuned to local climate. The importance of energy conservation and of climatic appropriateness are thus among the premises of an emergent solar energy discipline.

The Homegrown Sundwellings concept takes these concerns beyond the range of comfort and costs to an ethical issue. To construct using renewable resources is not a sentimental fad in an area without exportable products to pay for imports. To build and live in accord with nature in a region considered economically underdeveloped is not wistful romanticism but a question of the style of survival. In a low cash economy it is the interactions of human resources with the immediate materials of the land that provide for the richness and fullness of life. Sundwellings are not just thermally efficient building shells. They are the comprehensive expression of a complete way of life.

Although the Sundwellings program is based on extending a living tradition through active demonstration, this handbook provides no crisp formulas. It is not a "cookbook" of house design recipes. Nor does it provide ideal model plans. But by demystifying the sometimes scientific overtones of solar applications it provides a clear introduction to the thermal basis of building design that is now known as *passive solar.* The idea of a simpler, cheaper dwelling that is both longer lasting and more fulfilling is a universal goal shared by Sundwellings.

Scientific researchers will be amazed that so much has been accomplished on such a modest budget. Sociologists will be pleased with the degree to which this housing solution is based on human interactions. The self-confident will admire the streak of self-reliance that provides both manual muscle and ethical sinew to Homegrown Sundwellings. Architects and engineers who, in spite of the best of intentions, have seldom effected much impact on the fundamental problem of satisfactorily housing humanity will be delighted by the integration of principles where the total building becomes an instrument of comfort. Urban readers will surely suspect that the rural context of these proposals romantically avoids the issues of a postindustrial society. In fact, Sundwellings benefit from a region neglected by industrialization. Some would call it a rural slum. But an overlooked backwater of industrialization may be precisely the nesting ground for a vanguard of postindustrial prototypes—both in dwelling concepts and in settlement patterns.

The dwelling is the nest egg of society. The integrity of climatic and socioeconomic principles within the design of a dwelling is also the key to the integrity of a region. Home is where the hearth is. It is the place of genesis of human values and the repository of life's joy. It is also the generator of community. For its region Sundwellings would secure a complete future and a model of ecological and human integrity.

JEFFREY COOK
College of Architecture
Arizona State University

Preface

THE SUNDWELLINGS PROGRAM of which this publication is an outgrowth, was launched in mid-1974 by the Four Corners Regional Commission. It was conceived as a means of working with and strengthening the grassroots movement in New Mexico towards self-help solutions to the mounting problems of shelter, energy and food shortages. Intelligent use of universally available natural resources (mainly sun, earth and timber), and of the traditional skills of the citizenry, were the keynotes of this movement. It was hoped that systematic study of its achievements, coupled with a measure of technical analysis in the light of modern scientific developments in solar architecture and related technology, would help enrich this movement and increase its effectiveness in coping with the basic economic problems of many people in the State.

The funding (in the amount of $34,000 over a two-year period—see Appendix A) was channeled and administered through the Ghost Ranch Conference Center near Abiquiu in the Chama Valley sector of Rio Arriba County. The reasons for this were severalfold. The Ranch is a non-profit institution with a long-standing record of integrity. It is situated pretty much in the heart of the extensive northern New Mexico uplands region where the tradition of self-sufficiency and basic livelihood skills is still strong. And the Ranch staff has considerable experience in administering cooperative programs with local people in such fields as ranch management, animal husbandry, craft training and village development.

Under the general supervision of the administrative staff

of the Ranch, the Sundwellings program was placed in the hands of a team consisting of engineer-physicists, architects, and solar researchers and experimenters—most with long-term concern in this field and a personal familiarity with life and livelihood in rural and village New Mexico. Various consultants were also involved from time to time.

The total output of this team, during the scant two years of its activity (much on a part-time basis), is embodied in technical papers, reports at conferences, and architectural drawings and schematics. Since the material is voluminous we have not attempted to use it in its entirety. A good deal, however, is contained in a series of quarterly reports and accompanying drawings prepared for the Four Corners Regional Commission and totals several hundred pages. They are also on file with the New Mexico Solar Energy Association. See Appendix B.

During this same period the team also designed and arranged for the funding—through the New Mexico Office of Manpower Administration—of a demonstration-training project for the construction of a small group of suntempered buildings of native material. These are being completely instrumented by the Los Alamos Scientific Laboratory. Thermal performance during several heating seasons will be studied exhaustively. This is probably the only research and training program of this kind in the nation.

At this writing some 20 young citizens of the region are being trained in the practice and theory of energy-conserving construction adapted to the needs and resources of New Mexico.

Besides these demonstration and test cottages, one complete dwelling was designed by the author in cooperation with the team and is under construction. This dwelling is situated in the village of El Rito, Rio Arriba County, New Mexico, and, although privately financed, has been modestly subsidized by the Four Corners Regional Commission. It will be open to the public during and after construction on the first and last Sundays of each month beginning April 1977 through March 1979 between the hours of 2 and 5 p.m. See Appendix C for this and other house designs.

We trust this handbook will make a useful contribution towards grassroots competence in low-cost, energy-conserving, self-help livelihood techniques in our own State and wherever else in the world suitable conditions exist.

PETER VAN DRESSER

Santa Fe, New Mexico

February 10, 1977

Acknowledgments

The author hopes this text is an adequate summation of the creative and cooperative work of the Sundwellings team over the better part of two years. Their sympathetic and careful criticism of the text has been an essential factor and is highly valued.

Members of the Sundwellings team were:

Keith Haggard	Executive Director of the New Mexico Solar Energy Association
William Lumpkins	Santa Fe Architect
Aubrey Owen	Community Development Coordinator for Ghost Ranch
B. T. Rogers	Consulting Engineer to the Los Alamos Scientific Laboratories
Peter van Dresser	Associate Executive Director of the New Mexico Solar Energy Association
Francis Wessling	Professor of Mechanical Engineering at the University of New Mexico
David Wright	Architect and Builder

Douglas Balcomb, President of the New Mexico Solar Energy Association, and Jeffrey Cook, Department of Architecture at Arizona State University in Tempe, Arizona, nonmembers of the Sundwellings team, also reviewed the text and drawings contained herein. Their advice is much appreciated.

CETA (Comprehensive Employment Training Act) provided the Sundwellings team with the services of Mark Chalom who was an architectural assistant for the duration of the program.

Several people worked on graphics for the book. In alphabetical order, they are:

Mark Chalom, who illustrated the demonstration houses designed by the Sundwellings team;

Bruce Davis, who illustrated all of the figures within the text of the book, excepting the Appendices;

Lilibeth Harris, who illustrated the three solar crop driers and drew the cartoon on page 21;

Eugene V. Harris, who took the photographs;

William Lumpkins, who rendered the composite ideas of the Sundwellings design team into the schematics for an expandable prototype suntempered home, shown in Appendix C. He also prepared the schematics for the experimental solar house designed by the author, and "edited" by the Sundwellings team, also seen in Appendix C.

Typing and minor editing of this book were by Florence van Dresser.

PASSIVE
SOLAR HOUSE
BASICS

Solar Energy
A Natural for the Southwest

In the face of ever-mounting costs of fuel gas, fuel oil, and electricity, more and more people are giving serious thought to using solar energy in their struggle to make ends meet.

In the Southwest—particularly in the uplands and mountainous regions—solar energy makes good sense. These regions have severe winters which make it difficult to keep our homes and workplaces warm. Yet we live under a flood of warmth-bearing sunlight unmatched in most parts of the country. We also have a strong

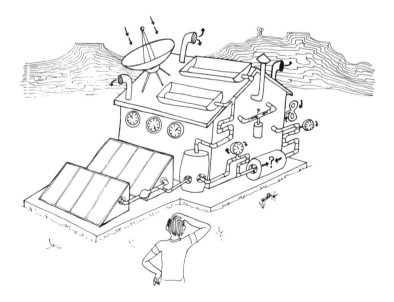

tradition of building competently in harmony with nature using simple native materials. The abundant sunshine and simple building materials have helped the Southwest, in recent years, to become one of the world centers for experimentation in the use of solar energy, particularly at the grassroots level of home heating. Within the past few years several dozen dwellings using solar input for a substantial portion of their energy requirements have been built in Arizona and New Mexico. The number increases each year.

We are still at a very early stage of solar energy use. For many the subject of solar heating remains a mysterious, difficult, yet desirable possibility. There is still a widespread impression that solar heating is a complicated matter of large aluminum, copper, and glass structures, intricate piping and electronic controls which require an engineer to understand and operate and a financier to pay for.

It is the main purpose of this book to correct this impression and to show how solar energy can be harnessed by simple means to ease the burden of living costs in the home. The methods are well within the grasp of average homeowners and home builders. A second purpose is to demonstrate how the Southwest's climate, natural resources, traditional customs, and lifestyles are particularly favorable to the methods explained herein. A third purpose is to show how the widespread use of renewable energy sources can make a substantial contribution towards easing the energy crisis and towards improving economic conditions, particularly among lower income people. This book also shows how these same methods can help protect the lands, waters, and atmosphere against the increasing menace of pollution.

Saving Fuel at the Home Front

WE BEGIN THIS DEMONSTRATION with some statistics.* At the national level the production of heat within our homes—in the form of space heating and hot water—consumes 14% of our entire energy budget. The sources are gas, oil, coal, hydro or nuclear power. In New Mexico this percentage is around 10%, but it still results in an overall figure of 29.1 "T.B.T.U.s" per year for residential heat and hot water. (One T.B.T.U. = one *trillion* British thermal units, a standard measure of heat energy.) For present purposes, it may suffice to say that to produce 29.1 trillion B.T.U.s—29,100,000,000,000—it is necessary to burn 29 billion cubic feet of natural gas, 290 million gallons of butane-propane or to consume 9 billion kilowatt hours of electricity. Our household heat requirements can eventually be reduced one-half to two-thirds by relatively simple changes and improvements in our home design and building practices, resulting in an annual savings of between $20 million to $30 million, if we figure costs in terms of natural gas, our most commonly used fuel. What these dollar figures may amount to 10 or 20 years from now hardly bears thinking about.

But how can our average homeowner and home builder begin to realize such savings?

Generally speaking, there are two courses of action:

(1) The most obvious is to improve the weather-tightness and insulating qualities of existing homes so that whatever

---

*Sources: *Patterns of Energy Consumption in the United States,* Stanford Research Institute; *Rocky Mountain Energy Flows,* Los Alamos Scientific Laboratories, 1974.

fuel we burn in our furnaces, heaters or stoves will give the best results at the lowest costs. The measures to accomplish this are pretty well known to practical builders and to many homeowners. For existing houses, they include weatherstripping, caulking of cracks, storm windows, insulating fill or blanket for ceilings, walls, and crawl spaces, as well as more careful attention to household management, such as thermostat settings, the closing of curtains or shutters, and the proper maintenance and adjustment of fuel-burning appliances. It is not a principal purpose of this study to give instruction in these procedures, as a large and growing literature is available, either in the form of pamphlets put out by various government agencies or by privately published books.*

According to statements in this literature fuel savings of up to one-third or even more may be accomplished by competent application of these simple measures and at costs which will be repaid by fuel bill savings in a few years.

Similarly, in the matter of improving the weather tightness and insulating values of new conventional homes built by the building industry, this study will not attempt a detailed discussion. Again, much attention is being paid to this subject by government agencies and by construction trade organizations. There appears to be a growing consensus that standards for thermal performance of typical speculatively or commercially built residences have been sacrificed in the past for low *first* costs and that these standards must be considerably upgraded to meet the mounting scarcity of cheap energy.

(2) The second major course of action to achieve effective energy conservation in our homes—and probably by far

---

*Some titles are: *Low Cost Energy Efficient Shelters*, by Eccli, Rodale Press, $5.95; *In the Bank or Up the Chimney?* U.S. Department of Housing and Urban Development, G.P.O. No. HH1-6 3: #N2/3, $1.70; *Save Energy, Save Money*, Office of Economic Opportunity, Pamphlet No. 6143-5; *Tips for Energy Savers*, Federal Energy Administration, Washington, D.C. 20461; *Your Energy Efficient House*, Garden Way Publishing, Charlotte, Vermont, $4.85. Through "Project Conserve," the New Mexico Energy Resources Board maintains a computerized service to homeowners which can analyze the thermal performance of individual homes and provide recommendations for improvement.

the most important in the long run—must be the development of the art of building dwellings which (a) work with and draw upon natural forces such as solar radiation, gravity flow, wind movements and the like, for a large proportion of their energy requirements and which (b) also require the least amount of "high-energy" manufactured materials for their construction. In this way we may become increasingly independent of costly, polluting and potentially dangerous commercial and industrial sources of power. To contribute to the development of this art, with particular reference to conditions in much of New Mexico, is the prime purpose of this book.

Some Principles of Climatic Adaptation

WE MIGHT SPEAK OF SUCH energy-saving dwellings as climatically or ecologically adapted, but the term solar is probably the most meaningful to the average person at present. Although this is an oversimplification, solar radiation is probably the most dominant single factor in the design and functioning of the new breed of energy-conserving dwelling. We might, therefore, begin with some elementary considerations on this subject.

The first point to notice is that every square foot of the earth's surface receives an annual quota of sunshine which carries with it a continuous flow or input of energy. The intensity, frequency and total amount of this energy flow vary, of course, from place to place, depending on factors such as latitude, the seasons, the alternation of day and night, the amount of cloud cover, etc. In the United States, the average of this annual energy flow for a year varies fairly widely: for example, from about 700,000 B.T.U.s in central Arizona and southern New Mexico to about 493,000 in Montana. If we visualize a well-insulated American single-story house of about 1,800 square feet ground area in each of these two locations, by simple multiplication we find that the site on which the house is built receives each year the impressive total of 1,260,000,000 B.T.U.s in Arizona or southern New Mexico, and 887,000,000 in Montana. (An average household furnace is capable of putting out about 100,000 B.T.U.s per hour, by way of comparison. To avoid the excessive amounts of zeros needed to express household heating requirements in this unit, we shall from here on use the "therm," consisting of 100,000 B.T.U.s. Thus, the average furnace would be rated at 1 therm per hour, and the annual solar input on the two house sites would be 12,600 therms and 8,870 therms, respectively.) *

The annual heating requirements of the two houses would vary considerably more than the available annual solar input, however. If we assume them to have average good weather tightness and insulating value, the house in Montana would require something like 1,728 therms of furnace-generated energy per heating season, while the one in Arizona would require only 389. But even in Montana, the theoretical solar input would exceed the heating requirements by a factor of 8570/1728, ** or about 4.9 times, while in southern New Mexico or central Arizona, the solar input would exceed heating needs 32 times. (The same house in the vicinity of Santa Fe, New Mexico, would receive about 9 times its heating requirement in annual solar input.***)

If this is true, why are fuel-burning furnaces and heaters so universal in our communities? Why is our per capita consumption of fossil fuel the greatest in the world and growing more so? Why are oil pipelines, fuel allotments, gas rationing and price controls such urgent political issues in our lives? Why, in New Mexico in particular, are not a good portion of

---

*Insolation data from *Climatic Atlas of the United States,* Environmental Science Service Administration, U.S. Department of Commerce table on page 70: Phoenix, Arizona, 520 Langleys $\times$ 365 $\times$ 3.69 = 700,000 B.T.U./ft.^{2} (horizontal); Santa Fe, New Mexico, 500 Langleys $\times$ 365 $\times$ 3.69 = 673,000 B.T.U./ft.^{2} (horizontal); Great Falls, Montana, 366 Langleys $\times$ 365 $\times$ 3.69 = 493,000 B.T.U./ft.^{2} (horizontal). Annual total on 1,800 ft.^{2}: Arizona: 700,000 $\times$ 1,800 = 1,260,000,000 B.T.U. = 12,600 therms; Montana: 493,000 $\times$ 1,800 = 887,000,000 B.T.U. = 8,870 therms; north central New Mexico: 673,000 $\times$ 1,800 = 1,211,000,000 B.T.U. = 12,110 therms.

**Arizona 1,800 degree days $\times$ 12 B.T.U./ft.^{2} $\times$ 1,800 ft.^{2} = 389 therms; Montana 8,000 $\times$ 12 $\times$ 1,800 = 1,728 therms; Santa Fe 5,300 $\times$ 12 $\times$ 1,800 = 1,444 therms.

***Heating load calculated by multiplying floor area times 12 B.T.U. times number of degree days at site, assuming average heat loss of 12 B.T.U./sq. ft./degree day with interior temperature maintained at 68° F.

our quarter of a million non-urban homes at least running on free solar energy independent of these vexing problems?

The simplest and most obvious reason is the inherently poor timing of solar input in relation to heating needs. During the winter months, sunshine intensity and amount drop off substantially, particularly in northerly latitudes due to the geometry of the earth's movement and tilt around the sun, and also to the greater likelihood of storminess and cloud cover. Figure 1 graphs the solar energy received by our 1,800 square-foot building site in south central Arizona, in north central New Mexico, and in Montana, on a month-to-month basis. It also shows the corresponding variations in the heat energy demands of the typical house built on these sites. The drastic drop-off of

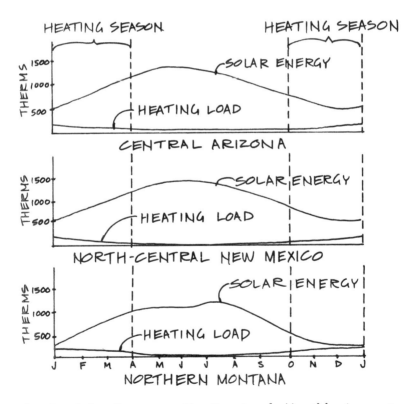

Fig. 1 Solar Energy vs Heating Load—Monthly Amounts at Three 1,800 Ft.² Sites

solar input at the time when heating needs reach their maximum shows up clearly in these graphs and is, in any case, a matter of common knowledge. What the graphs also show, however, which is not such common knowledge, is that even during the winter season, the total solar input on the sites still exceeds the heating requirements. For south central Arizona, as would be expected, this surplus is generous, amounting to about 24 times. For north central New Mexico, it is reduced to 10 times, and for Montana it is a marginal 2.6.

But we cannot allow ourselves to become unduly encouraged by these highly generalized statistics. While the winter total of solar energy on our site may be several times our total house-heating requirements for the same period, there are other shorter-term variations in the relationship which make it difficult to draw upon this source of energy. The most obvious is the day-to-night variation. In winter, there is effective sunshine for only six or seven hours out of each 24. Additionally, there are periods of cloudiness lasting from a day to more than a week, during which solar radiation is negligible and air temperatures may be frigid. These periods are perhaps the most difficult to cope with as they are irregular in occurrence and very much dependent on local weather conditions. With conventional heating systems, we cope with them by firing up our furnaces or heaters, thus drawing upon the stored and concentrated solar energy in gas, oil, coal or wood. To devise methods for drawing upon stored *direct* solar energy for the same purpose requires novel arrangements and techniques whose perfection is a real challenge and one which we are just beginning to think about seriously.

Requirements for the House as Solar Energy Transformer

To MEET THIS CHALLENGE we attempt to design and build our dwellings so that they will:

(1) receive and absorb solar radiation as effectively as possible whenever it is available during the months of cold weather;

(2) store the energy in this radiation in such a way that it can be drawn upon during periods of greatest need;

(3) reduce to a minimum overall heating requirements by attention to such details as the general shape and proportion of the house, its placing and orientation on the site, the tightness of its construction, and the selection and use of the materials of which it is built, with particular reference to their abilities to absorb, transmit, insulate, or store heat; and

(4) meet these requirements at costs we can afford and with the least amount of complicated equipment and materials which require much energy for their manufacture and transport.

We will now examine in more detail the four requirements for the house as solar energy transformer.

REQUIREMENT ONE—Effective Absorption and Reception of Solar Radiation

This is a matter of exposing a large and efficiently absorbing surface to the sun's winter rays and of shaping and fitting the house to best receive and hold the resulting warmth. The time-honored device for this purpose is, of course, the south-facing window which, in the form of bays, sunporches, etc., has been used by generations of architects and home builders to bring the cheer of sunshine and some measure of its warmth into interior living spaces. A suntempered house may be thought of as one in which the south-facing window—or some equivalent arrangement—has been enlarged and perfected to the highest degree practicable, so that it is no longer a mere auxiliary to warmth and comfort, but the principal source of it.

In more specific terms this means designing a house with a generous southern exposure or facade and a minimal heat-losing surface to the north. In its most elementary form this results in the familiar shed cross section with a relatively high southern wall carrying large windows which permit the lower winter sun to flood the interior of the house through a good part of the day (Figure 2).

The design and arrangement of these large solar-intake windows and their auxiliaries are of considerable importance to the success of the suntempering system. Probably the first choice to be made is between double-glazing and the provision of tight-fitting insulating shutters or closures of some sort. Double-glazing is, of course, generally desirable in most cases but over large expanses it can be quite costly. Well-fitted and well-insulated outside shutters, if consistently closed at night and during cold and heavily overcast weather, can greatly reduce the heat loss through these large glass expanses and can, in fact, bring the overall thermal performance of the windows quite close to double-glazed installations. On the other hand, the placing, mounting, and hinging of such large units can make an awkward problem. One of the most mechanically and thermally effective solutions is the drawbridge type hatch, hinged at the bottom and lying flat on the ground in front of the window when open. If lined with a reflective surface (as aluminum foil), such hatches can bounce extra sunlight into the windows and thus increase the solar intake. They are apt, however, to dominate the architectural character of the south facade of the house and create a mechanical and gadgety impression which many find distasteful. In any case, they should probably best be used in connection with some version of a "Trombe" wall (so named for the physicist-inventor of the famous solar fur-

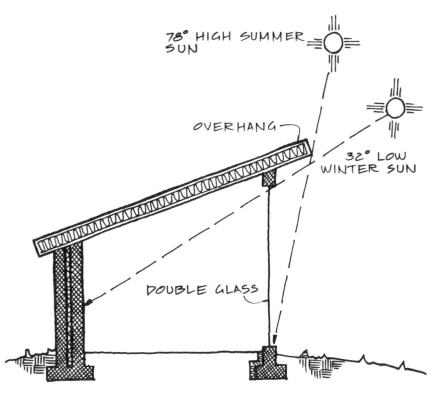

78° HIGH SUMMER SUN

OVERHANG

32° LOW WINTER SUN

DOUBLE GLASS

NORTH LOW   SOUTH HIGH

Fig. 2 Shed Roof House—Cross Section

nace research installation in the French Pyrenees) or "water-wall." The glare they reflect into the house, through simple direct gain windows, would frequently be unpleasant.

More conventional vertically hinged exterior shutters avoid these esthetic drawbacks. However, to close large openings and still not take up too much space when folded back, they have to be double-hinged and in sections, which adds to the difficulties of fabrication and securing tight joints. And, of course, they must be worked from outside, which some might find a disagreeable chore on a cold winter evening.

Interior shutters avoid this last objection, but they offer the same problem of providing sufficient blank wall space against which they may be folded when not in use. They also complicate the placing of furniture. Lastly, the glass in a window closed off from inside becomes deeply chilled during winter nights so that heavy frost deposits form and are apt to melt into sizable trickles of water when the shutters are opened in the morning.

Heavy interior curtains or drapes are frequently proposed as an alternative solution. These avoid the problems of hinging and folding-back space and of interference with furniture. For situations where the maximum in thermal efficiency is not required, they probably offer a reasonable compromise. Even so, they should be very carefully tailored of double interlined design. The interlining might well be of some airtight reflective fabric. Special care should be taken that they seal effectively when closed, especially at the top, probably by means of a valance enclosure. Top and bottom leakage will cause the space between curtain and glass to act as a chimney in reverse, down which a current of chilling air will flow all night, effectively draining the room of warmth. (The same caution applies, of course, to the installation of interior shutters. They must fit tightly at top and bottom.)

Various modifications of this basic cross section are possible, as through a stepped cross section with high or clerestory windows permitting sunlight to enter towards the back of the house (Figure 3).

All of these south solar windows should be provided with an eave overhang proportioned to cut off most of the rays of the high summer sun. Skylights may be employed to some extent to reinforce the solar intake in certain locations, but these should be used with caution by home builders, as they involve problems of water-tightness, night closing and summer shading which are more readily handled in wall-mounted windows. This general caution applies in fact to any expanse of horizontal or nearly horizontal glass used as roof for a patio, sunporch, greenhouse, interior atrium, etc. The heat loss to the night sky from such transparent expanses will usually exceed what they gain during sunny days considerably unless thorough arrangements for insulating closures are provided.

This whole approach to solar intake has come to be called the "direct gain" system.

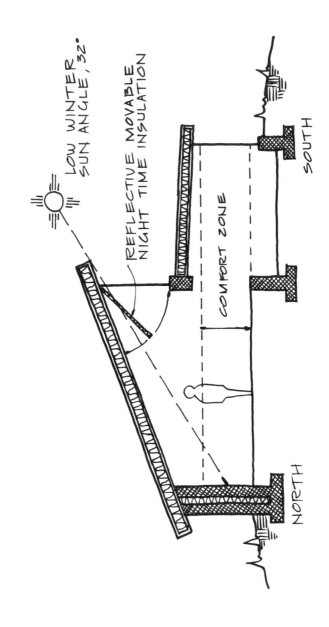

Fig. 3 Clerestory Gain—Cross Section

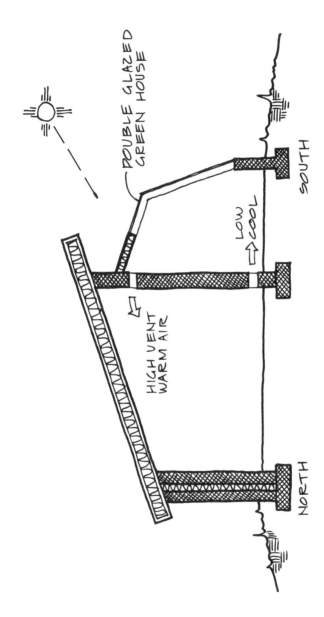

Fig. 4 Lean-to Greenhouse—Cross Section

The bank of south-facing solar (or direct gain) windows may be wholly or partially replaced by a lean-to greenhouse (Figure 4). In this case, air warmed during the day within the greenhouse is circulated into the main house through high vents and cool air is returned to the greenhouse through correspond-

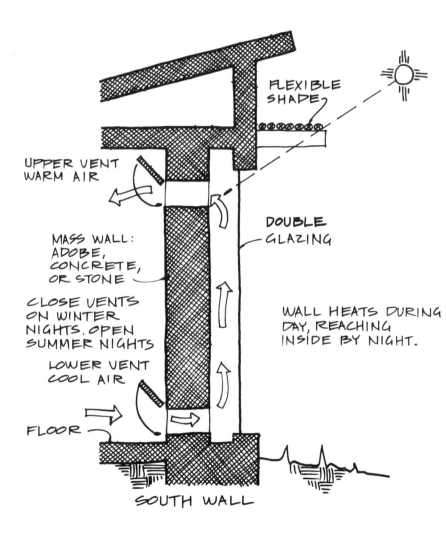

Fig. 5 Trombe Wall—Cross Section

ing floor-level vents or underfloor ducts. This circulation may be speeded up by low-wattage fans, but the vents should be closed at night. Even on cold nights at elevations up to about 8,000 feet in north central New Mexico, a properly designed greenhouse with partial roof cover, some storage, and double-glazing will normally maintain not less than 40° F., which is adequate for many plants, and the heat it has generated during the day will make a substantial contribution to the energy budget of the main house. At higher elevations, or unusually cold locations, it may be necessary to provide some form of insulating closure for the greenhouse.

Part of the south facade may be designed as a Trombe wall (Figure 5) rather than a solar window. This combines the function of solar intake and heat storage and, while probably not quite so efficient in overall performance as a well-designed and properly operated direct gain installation, is desirable for certain purposes, as in rooms where the light and lack of privacy of large solar windows may be excessive. It is also well suited for adapting some existing houses to solar assistance.

REQUIREMENT TWO—Storage of Solar Radiation Energy

The requirement for the storage of daytime peaks of solar intake for slow release at night or on cloudy days may be handled surprisingly effectively by simple arrangements other than large liquid reservoirs or rock-filled silos which more elaborate solar heating systems employ. The basic strategy is to design the house so that its own masses—mainly walls and floors—are so placed, proportioned, and surfaced that they will receive and store a large measure of incoming solar energy during the daylight hours and will gently release this stored heat to the house interior during the succeeding night hours or cloudy days. This requirement, along with that for opening up the south exposure to incoming sunlight, must obviously have a large influence on the plan and layout of the house.

Before we begin the discussion of this plan and layout, it may be generally noted that adobe, the traditional construction material of native New Mexican homes, is very well suited to this heat-storage task. Our average 1,800 square foot home, if built of 14 inch thick adobe block (including interior partitions), may easily weigh in the vicinity of up to 150 tons in the walls alone, and this mass of material, even if only slightly warmed, will store very large quantities of heat.

Reverting to the basic solar shed cross section shown in Figure 2, it is clear that the floor in such a structure receives much of the incoming sunlight. It is therefore logical to deliberately design this floor as one of the prime absorbers and storers of sun-generated heat. Again, for this purpose, a traditional New Mexican floor—either of treated and filled adobe clay or of brick or flagstone laid over sand—is very well suited. Its rich dark color makes it a good absorber of radiation; its moderate conductivity permits the heat to travel slowly down into its body; and its sheer mass gives it great capacity to store this heat with a very slight rise in temperature. If we visualize such a floor 12 inches deep in a room 16 feet square with one exterior wall and an average window, warmed to a mere 72° F. (just slightly warm to the touch), it will store 40,000 B.T.U.s of heat, which will be released into the room as it cools down to, say, 65° F. This is sufficient heat to take care of a well-insulated room for 26 hours, with an outdoor temperature of, say, 20°. Actually the bulk of heat storage for release over the dark period of the 24-hour daily cycle, will occur in the top 6 inches of such a slab floor. Heat which penetrates deeper than this will be available for longer periods of cloudiness.

To allow the floor to act in this fashion: (a) it must be well-exposed to incoming sunlight (eliminating wall-to-wall carpeting and too much clutter of furniture); and (b) it must be well-insulated against heat leakage into the surrounding earth. This leakage is particularly active around the outer edges of the building and is guarded against by an insulating barrier alongside the footings carried down to a depth of about 2 feet (Figure 6). This has come to be called perimeter insulation and is now often formed of styrofoam, although waterproofed celotex is much used. Though some designers feel that this insulating barrier should be continued underneath the entire floor mass, the need for this is not established as heat which travels a few feet down into the earth below the house is not lost to useful purpose and still contributes to the reservoir of warmth underneath the building. The manufactured slabs of styrofoam or fiber may be replaced by pumice-filled trenches or beds which must be five or six times as thick as the slabs to achieve equivalent insulating value.

High-water table or moisture underneath the house will nullify the effectiveness of most insulation and must be guarded against. The surest remedy is not to build on poorly drained sites—especially *cienegas* or fields in which the water table rises with the spring runoff—a condition fairly common in much of rural New Mexico. If a site of this kind is unavoidable,

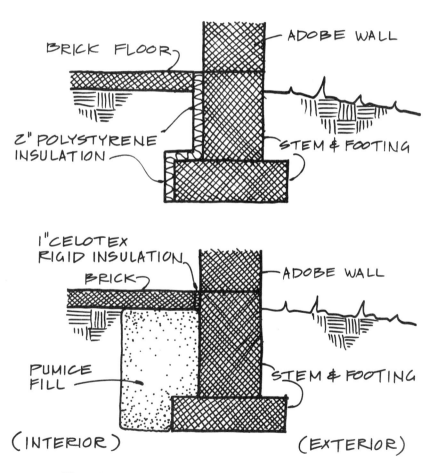

Fig. 6   Perimeter Insulation—Cross Sections

special precautions must be taken. French drains—gravel-filled trenches pitched to carry away subsurface water—may have to be constructed outside the footings. A bed of gravel may have to be laid underneath the main floor mass and sealed off from it by a heavy-duty membrane of plastic. The tops of the concrete stem walls on which the adobe wall blocks are laid should be sealed with asphalt to prevent capillary action from drawing moisture up into the lower courses of the block.

The next most important heat storage mass in the house is made up of walls and partitions. These are usually not so well placed to receive incoming sunlight as is the floor, although with some clerestory window arrangements, a portion of this may be directed onto rear walls (Figure 3). However, any interior wall surface can pick up and absorb a good measure of warmth radiated or reflected from the floor in the form of both light and invisible low-temperature infrared rays, and also from the gentle natural circulation of warmed air within the house. As suggested earlier, a few degrees rise in temperature of the wall masses from this source can represent a large reserve of stored warmth. (The famed summer and winter comfort of a well-built and properly laid out adobe house comes mainly from this ability and not from its supposed insulating qualities which, in fact, are only fair-to-poor when rated against other insulating materials.) Again, as in the case of perimeter insulation for floors and footings, the strategy here is to guard against leakage of this stored heat to the outside mainly, of course, in the case of exterior walls. The defense against this is to: (a) reduce to a minimum the area of exposed non-south-facing walls (especially to the north); and (b) insulate in some way the outside of exterior walls which receive little or no sunlight. The basic shed cross section discussed earlier, and various modifications of it, accomplish point (a) by reducing the height and area of the north wall. This effect may be further enhanced by digging back into a south-facing slope so that the north side of the house is partially underground and the area of exposed north wall still further reduced.

The exterior insulation of adobe walls remains something of a problem. The recent advent of foamed plastic slabs is leading to the use of such slabs as an external insulating jacket. In one system the slabs are fastened to the adobe by long nails and covered with tightly stretched poultry mesh over tarpaper (as is done for an ordinary exterior stuccoing job) and the usual coats of portland cement exterior plaster are applied to this. The result can be indistinguishable from normal adobe exterior finishes and produces a very good insulating jacket. The drawbacks are expense, the dependence on a high-energy manufactured material whose production is part of the national pollution problem, and some question as to the permanence of such an installation, as the practice is still quite new. One should be aware that some of the plastics used give off highly poisonous vapors in case of fire.

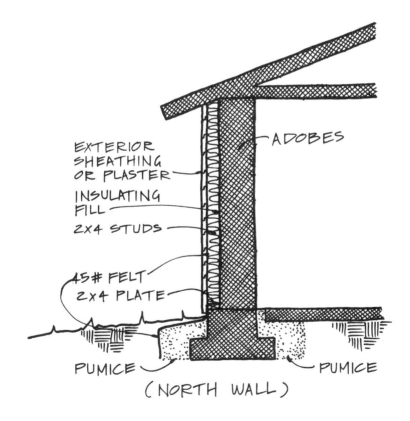

EXTERIOR
SHEATHING
OR PLASTER

ADOBES

INSULATING
FILL

2X4 STUDS

45# FELT

2X4 PLATE

PUMICE

PUMICE

(NORTH WALL)

Fig. 7 Exterior Insulating Furring—Cross Section

Alternatives could be the construction of an *exterior* furred space filled with some such insulating material as perlite, shredded fiber or sawdust (Figure 7). This exterior furring would, of course, have to be well-sealed and protected by the eave overhang. Perhaps the most practical solution for the rural New Mexico home builder is a double exterior adobe wall (at least on the north side) with a 6 or 8 inch interior space filled with pumice or perlite. The exterior course of adobe could be minimum in thickness—even 10 inches—while the interior course, which forms a part of the heat storage system of the house, should be thicker—probably the customary 14 inches.

The question inevitably comes up at this point as to the effectiveness of walls entirely formed of some lightweight semi-insulating masonry material. The most common form of this in New Mexico is pumice block, but a number of people are experimenting with various poured or rammed mixtures of pumice, earth, and sand with a small proportion of portland cement. Though walls of this nature can be satisfactory in many respects, their thermal properties do not particularly work with the needs of the passive, climatically adapted house outlined above. For one thing, their density and the resulting overall mass are relatively low, hence the important capacity to store heat is reduced. Again, their relatively good insulating quality prevents them from absorbing heat and conducting it uniformly through their mass, which is essential for smoothing out the variations in solar input. Houses built of such materials (and also of good, well-insulated wood framing) can perform well at containing fuel-generated heat, but as solar structures are apt to require more elaborate systems than the simple measures discussed in this book.

Finally, a method of externally insulating the house is to bank earth against the non-solar walls, particularly north. This has come to be called bermed construction and, although somewhat unconventional, if well-designed and executed, can be pleasing to the eye. A drawback is that this bermed wall must be reinforced to carry the extra burden of earth.

The inherent heat-bank capacities of the normal floors, walls and partitions which compose the dwellings can be backed up by various special arrangements which are still passive in nature. One highly publicized system uses tiers of water-filled containers (usually 55-gallon steel drums) stacked to receive incoming sunlight through the south solar windows (Figure 8). Such "waterwalls" or "drumwalls" have a considerably greater capacity to store heat, in proportion to their weight and volume, than equivalent masonry or adobe masses. Moreover, the natural circulation of the water within each container provides an efficient means of distributing the solar heat received on the exposed surface of the container uniformly throughout the volume of water. Drawbacks are the difficulty of fitting such tiers of containers pleasingly into the interior of a dwelling, the increasing cost and scarcity of the necessary drums or other containers and some question as to what trouble-free lifetime can be expected before minor seeps and leaks become a problem. Use of rust inhibitors, neutralizing agents and special coatings can no doubt extend this life expectancy, but these further increase expense. In any case, working knowledge of the subject is somewhat limited at this writing. It should be noted that large manufactured plastic containers are now coming on the market for this purpose, but their use is not particularly consonant with the "homegrown," low-energy philosophy of this study.

The Trombe wall mentioned earlier is a combination solar receptor and heat storage arrangement that meets our requirements for simplicity and feasibility of local construction. In essence, this is a south-facing masonry wall with a glazed air space on its outer surface. Protected by this glazing from direct contact with the cold outside air and from heat loss through invisible heat radiation to the exterior, the wall becomes much hotter—and absorbs more energy—than if it were simply exposed to the sun. The effect is increased by double-glazing and by coloring the outer surface of the wall with a dark absorbing pigment. The absorbed heat penetrates the interior of the wall and eventually reaches the interior of the house, which it continues to warm long after the sun has set. Additionally, vents are provided at the top and bottom of the wall so that a part of the absorbed solar heat enters the interior directly in the form of warm air. There is some evidence that due to its higher conductivity and density, concrete or stone masonry is a better material for this type of wall than adobe.

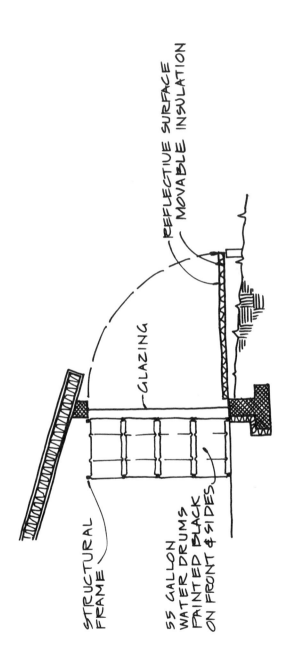

Fig. 8 Waterwall or Drumwall—Cross Section

Figure 5 illustrates a typical cross section of such an installation. Properly designed and built, it may add about 500 B.T.U.s per day per square foot of its surface to the interior space it faces. This is less than the input of an equivalent area or direct gain solar window, provided the latter is closed at night with effective insulating shutters.

REQUIREMENT THREE—Shaping and Siting the House for Climatic and Thermal Efficiency

A number of experimenters with solar-assisted dwellings have assumed that the best shape for such a structure is round or polygonal, or something approaching this form. The dome is the most complete version of this idea which springs from the simple principle that this shape encloses the most space or volume with the least amount of exterior—and potentially heat-losing—surface. This is true as far as it goes and if one were building a habitation for use in the Arctic (or in outer space!), where survival depends entirely on an inner-contained source of energy for warmth, a dome or even a sphere would be the logical shape.

The dome or circular shape, however, is not well suited to the various climatic factors, especially solar input and seasonal variations, to which we wish our dwellings to be adapted. Some considerations of these factors and of building cross sections arising from them have been outlined earlier. Pursuing this subject further, we arrive at the perhaps prosaic conclusion that the typical passive suntempered building is roughly rectangular in plan, with its long axis running approximately east and west so that it provides a generous southern exposure. It is also somewhat shallow or narrow in its north-south dimension—usually one room deep so that the incoming sunlight through the solar windows may reach well into most of the living area. This linear or "string" arrangement of rooms has commonsense limitations, particularly as regards convenience of circulation within the building, and the increase of wall area in proportion to its volume which may increase construction costs. A reasonable compromise would be to fill out the building to a more nearly square plan by locating on the north side utility rooms, corridors, storerooms, pantries, workshops and other spaces which are used only occasionally, do not need to be warmed to the "comfort" level, or should be permanently cool. Some arrangements of this kind will be found amongst the schematic plans in this manual.

In regard to roofs, most of the design suggestions presented herein show sloping one-rake (shed) or gable roofs, rather than the traditional flat deck with surrounding parapet which is the older tradition in much of New Mexico. In a country lacking suitable native woods for shingle-making and with low average rainfall, the flat earth roof laid over *latias* (peeled or split cedar poles) carried on round log rafters or *vigas* was an ingenious adaptation to available materials. Such roofs, if sufficiently thick, were quite good weather stoppers and interior temperature regulators, but they required considerable patching and maintenance, particularly around the joints where the *canales* or scupper troughs pierced the parapet to carry off water. But as soon as galvanized iron became available—probably around 1890—homeowners in rural New Mexico began surmounting their flat roofs with gabled ones of corrugated iron which are by now a tradition of several generations' standing. From the standpoint of construction by local craftsmen, this still represents the most practical and enduring kind of roof. A secondary advantage of the pitched metal roof is its suitability for use as a rainwater and snowmelt collector in areas where ground water is scarce or lacking. Corrugated iron roofs which have been in place 50 years or more and are still in fairly good condition are common in the older villages and towns of the State.

It is true that, particularly in town and urban areas, the flat-roof deck has been perpetuated by the application of built-up membrane roofing techniques, but this is essentially a commercial process requiring specialized equipment. Where a home builder has access to a local roofer with such equipment, he may wish to design a traditional flat-roofed, parapeted house, but he will have difficulty achieving an insulating value equivalent to the other roof systems here outlined, and he must be prepared for continuous maintenance operations. An alternative might be to revert to the original primitive system of deep earth fill over a plank roof which is sealed with heavy tarpaper (a material not available to early pioneers). In this case local knowledge should be sought as to the best mix for the fill, to minimize seepage. The lifestyle of the homeowner will also be a factor in this choice. Heavy 90# slate-coated asphalt roofing felt laid on pitched lumber sheathing represents an alternative to sheet metal roofing for local use; it does not require the very thorough sealing techniques which are necessary with horizontal built-up membrane roofing.

As far as the solar-thermal performance of the dwellings is concerned, most of the roof forms sketched here are essentially neutral; they make no positive contribution of solar heat to the house, nor do they contribute much to the heat-storing mass of the structure. They do keep out the weather and also must provide the greatest possible insulation against heat leakage from the interior. This may be accomplished by the use of lightweight manufactured fiber or plastic insulating slabs laid over the roof sheathing before the waterproof outer skin is applied. This is a technique well understood by practical builders and roofers and need not be detailed here. However, in keeping with the native-materials, local-craftsmanship approach of this book, it must be pointed out that ceiling and roofing arrangements with excellent insulating properties may be built up of locally available low-cost materials. Figure 9 details such an arrangement.

Over a traditional ceiling of ponderosa planks (or even peeled cedar or oak *latias*) carried on *vigas,* there is placed an insulating fill of pumice, perlite or coarse sawdust. (The latter material has the best R-factor or insulating value of the three, averaging about two-thirds that of Fiberglas. According to the U.S. Forest Products Laboratory, its use as a fill in furred spaces is less of a fire hazard than leaving the spaces empty, and it is no more attractive to vermin than the empty space would be. It must, of course, be kept dry.) The fill material is kept from trickling into the room below by a membrane laid over the ceiling boards which may be lightweight roofing felt (tarpaper) or even building paper. Over this insulating fill, which should be 8 or 10 inches thick or more, if possible, the weather roof is carried on lightweight rafters (probably rough 2x4s) braced or strutted to the ceiling below. This weather roof may, as before indicated, be 90# slate-coated roofing paper laid over roofing felt on rough lumber sheathing or corrugated metal laid over scantlings. Its pitch should be no less

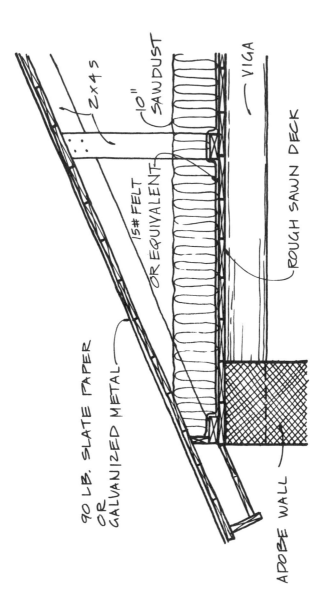

90 LB. SLATE PAPER OR GALVANIZED METAL

2 x 4 S

10" SAWDUST

15# FELT OR EQUIVALENT

VIGA

ROUGH SAWN DECK

ADOBE WALL

Fig. 9 Insulating Roof Section—Using Low-cost, Low-energy Locally Available Materials

than 1 in 4. The insulating value of such a combined roof and ceiling arrangement should be about R 25, which is equivalent to 6 or 7 inches of Fiberglas.

A good case can be made, however, for arranging the roof so that it becomes a positive contributor to the heat budget of the house through solar input and not simply a neutral insulator. It makes up, after all, the largest single surface exposed to the sun's rays and, if properly designed, should pick up a great deal of heat energy. This implies, first of all, a change in the basic shape of the house. Most of the direct gain plans call for roofs sloping downward from south to north, to provide the necessary high southern exposure. This faces the roof surface pretty much *away* from the low-angle winter sunlight and makes it a poor collector. A roof sloping the other way, *towards* the sun could, by contrast, act as a fairly efficient collector of very large area.

One way of accomplishing this is to cover the roof with galvanized sheet iron, providing an air space of an inch or an inch and a half between the metal and the roof sheathing. (The main body of roof insulation must, of course, be placed below this sheathing.) Warm air accumulating in this air space is allowed to rise towards the upper edge of the roof where it is collected by a suitable duct arrangement and forced downward into the house. Figure 10 diagrams the basics of this arrangement. There is evidence that this type of roof surface, *after it is weathered,* has surprisingly good absorbing properties for solar heat and, furthermore, is rather poor at reradiating the heat back to the sky. (This is known as the selective effect and has been the subject of some rather sophisticated research.)

Drawbacks of this system are: some electric power is required to operate the fans or blowers which suck the warm air downward into the house and through the storage bank, thus the system is not strictly passive although the wattage required can be low. Since the collector is not glass-covered to shield it from cooling by air currents, the efficiency of absorption is probably quite variable, being dependent on the windiness of the day. For this reason the system should probably be used in conjunction with some sort of rock storage bank to absorb the large output on still, sunny days and make up for the deficiency on windy days, as is shown in Figure 10. Not much data exists as to the performance of such roof collectors, although a laboratory built in 1959 near Tucson under Arizona State University auspices used its sheet copper roof as collector, and at least two houses are currently being built—one in Albuquerque and one in El Rito, Rio Arriba County—which will incorporate unglazed sheet metal roof collectors.

A house incorporating this system will depend less on the direct gain effect—the south facade and, hence, any solar windows installed there will be reduced in area due to the south slope of the roof. But there is no reason why the two methods cannot be combined. A secondary and, in some locations, an

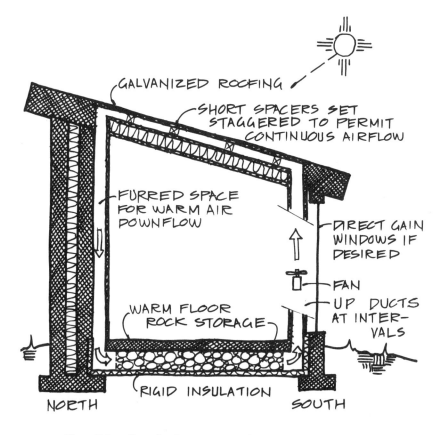

**Fig. 10 South-sloping Roof as Heat Collector—
Cross Section**

important asset of the south-sloping roof is its suitability for snowmelt collection. A gutter leading to a water-storage cistern (preferably underground), placed along the lower south eave of such a roof will have far less tendency to freeze than one on the north side, and accumulated snowpack will melt off much more freely.

Some potential home designers and builders at this point may feel that the prescriptions so far set forth are too restrictive and must result in stereotyped rectangular houses not much better than many mass-produced tract residences. This is particularly true for those interested in free-form habitat and in variations of the dome. In reply it may be pointed out that much range for creative design exists in combining and modifying the various functional shapes and surfaces so far discussed—by the use of clerestories, interior balconies, mezzanine floors, etc.—while the interior spaces need not be subdivided into the conventional bedroom-living room-kitchen pattern but may be opened up into newer concepts of combined many-purpose living-working-craft-growing spaces associated with less conventional lifestyles. Curved wall sections—in plan— are quite feasible in adobe and may be used, as may also be battering or sloping of walls, to soften contours and when they make good design sense.

Even the general prescription for east-west compass orientation has been successfully contradicted in at least one passive solar house which achieves ample direct gain input by climbing up a south slope and presenting a series of tiered clerestory windows to the sun. (See Figure 11.) The point should be insisted upon that domed, warped, hyperboloid and similar surfaces dear to avant-garde architects, *which must at the same time be rain- and weather-tight,* are very difficult to execute in low-energy indigenous materials. For their success they are dependent on the use of high-energy plastic membranes, sealers, foamed or sprayed fillers and coatings, aluminum extrusions, plywood and the like. Additionally, it is very difficult to incorporate weather-tight window openings and solar collecting panels into such curved or warped surfaces.

An exception to this generality would be the domes and vaults of Egyptian and Levantine folk adobe buildings, but these represent adaptations to a climate and lifestyle so different from ours that it is very difficult at this time to assess their relevancy.*

REQUIREMENT FOUR—Low Cost in Money and Energy

Virtually the entire range of recommendations so far made for achieving suntempered or climatically adapted dwellings is in line with this requirement. To sum them up: we utilize the simplest solar heating methods which require no machinery and no elaborate piping and depend principally on the way we lay out our houses and install windows, insulation, etc., and we

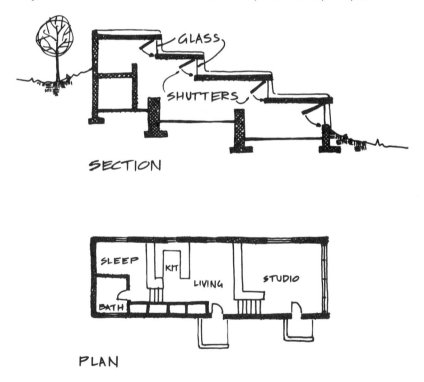

Fig. 11 North-South Oriented Direct Gain House

---

*The book, *Architecture for the Poor,* by the Egyptian architect Hassan Fathy, gives an excellent description of this type of folk domestic architecture. It was published by the University of Chicago Press.

substitute wherever possible low-cost, readily available local materials for prefabricated or manufactured products. Obviously this approach does not minimize the personal labor involved in building a house, but this is a responsibility which generations of New Mexicans have shouldered and which is still widely accepted. As an alternative to entrapment in the vicious spiral of inflation, indebtedness and mounting scarcities of industrial resources, this approach makes very good sense to many New Mexicans and is, fortunately, well adapted to the traditions, lifestyle and economic realities of many communities throughout the State.

Windows, Ventilation and Summer Comfort

SO FAR THE DISCUSSION has revolved about the problem of keeping warm in winter with the least possible fuel consumption—a serious consideration in much of the world. In New Mexico our seasonal cycle is very marked and our homes have always had to be built with the intense sunlight of summer and its occasional sequences of hot arid days in mind. Several factors tend to reduce the need for us to resort to mechanical air conditioning—a favorite but costly energy-consumptive device of the modern commercial construction industry.* The first of these factors is the rather marked difference in day and night temperature peaks even in midsummer. The second is the generally low humidity of the atmosphere. And the third is the fortunate fact that the traditional recipe for building construction in this kind of climate—massive walls and a well-insulated roof—works almost as well to maintain moderately low interior temperatures in summer as it does to maintain moderately high ones in winter. The well-insulated roof serves to block off the penetration of solar heat into the house from above, while the massive walls are capable of storing night coolth to temper the

---

*A modern air-conditioned house normally consumes about 40% as much energy for summer cooling as it requires for winter heating, according to a study made for the Housing and Urban Development Department on Residential Energy Consumption (HUD-HAI-2). In the south, the percentage may be considerably higher.

interior during the hot day, almost as well as they can store daytime warmth for release at night in winter.* In this connection it should be noted that the traditional earthfilled roof, while it is not so effective an insulator as other types herein discussed, has some advantages in regard to summer cooling. Its large heat storage capacity allows it to act as a heat sink during the day, intercepting and storing solar radiation so that its effects do not reach the interior of the house until evening.

These effects are not entirely automatic and should be strengthened as much as possible by proper building design. A most obvious consideration which has already been mentioned is the provision of an eave overhang at the south wall to shield the solar windows and the wall itself from direct sunlight during most of the summer day when the sun is high overhead. This feature is lacking in what has come to be regarded as the traditional flat-roofed, parapeted New Mexico home. It is often achieved by the provision of a *portal* or porch on the south side of the house—a welcome zone of shady coolness in summer, but one which often tends to block out the desirable warming rays in winter. It might be noted here that many really old buildings in New Mexico achieved the effect of an eave overhang by extending the roof *vigas* two or three feet out from the exterior walls and placing the parapet at this outer edge. From this arrangement derives the Spanish name, *pendal,* for the parapet, as one of the functions was to hold the roof *vigas* in place by sheer weight. This arrangement began to go out of style sometime around the 1920s.

An obvious commonsense need for summer comfort—but one which is sometimes neglected in these days of mechanical ventilation and air conditioning—is the provision of openable windows for adequate cross-ventilation.

---

*The Harold Hays system for climatically tempering buildings by the management of roof exposure to the sky is probably adapted to the hotter lower portion of New Mexico, but it is not included here as it requires industrial fabrications and is not well suited to the native-materials-and-craftsmanship approach called for in this book. It is described in packets which may be secured by sending a stamped self-addressed envelope to Skytherm Processes and Engineering Company, 2424 Wilshire Boulevard, Los Angeles, California 90057.

There are various more or less elaborate theories as to the placing of such windows to ensure adequate and continuous natural circulation of air through a house in summer weather. However, conditions vary so much from site to site, house to house, and with the vagaries of local weather that the ideal air-flow pattern supposed to be produced by any given scheme may be nullified or even reversed. Accordingly, only some simple generalizations will be attempted here and specific solutions left to local knowledge and the ingenuity of the home builder.

Any room occupied consistently in the summer should have at least two exposures with openable windows or should have some arrangement for cross-ventilation, as into an adjoining hallway. The Universal Building Code recommends that windows represent no less than ⅛ of the floor area of the room, with one-half of this window area openable.

Windows should be tall enough to reach from ordinary low sill height above the floor to within a couple of feet of the ceiling, so that they may pick up cool surface breezes or vent warm air from the upper part of the room.

Windows in west or northwest walls should be carefully shaded from the glare of late afternoon summer sun.

Windows in south walls must obviously be shaded from low summer sun throughout most of the day. South windows in a suntempered direct gain house present a special problem in that they must be somehow fitted into the large exposures of fixed double-glazing, Trombe wall or greenhouse which take up much of the south facade. Various design solutions can be found for this situation, mostly involving alternations of the large direct gain surfaces with smaller panels or bays of openable windows.

High windows, at balconies or in clerestories, may be useful in venting warm air from the upper part of the house. However, it must be borne in mind that such windows may actually scoop in hot winds under some conditions. If there is a consistent compass direction of warm summer breezes, such windows should be placed to face away from them.

Most windows in an energy-conserving house should be tightly closing and double-glazed. Windows in north walls may be profitably provided with storm sash in winter. It might be noted that the old-fashioned double-hung windows, if well made, show up very well in these respects. Since they may be opened either at top or bottom, they are flexible in their application and may serve to vent warm air on the lee side of the house or take in cool breezes on the windward side. While such windows have been almost forced off the commercial market by manufactured aluminum units, there are fortunately still small cabinet and millwork shops in New Mexico towns which can custom-build them at competitive prices, and the prospective energy-conserving home builder will do well to investigate this source. (See Figure 12.) The side benefits to the local economy of such small home-owned industries are apparent.

In any case windows for an effective energy-conserving house will not be of the cheapest sort, but extra investment of money or work in the most efficient type will repay itself over the years in fuel savings and comfort.

Passive solar-powered ventilation and cooling for small buildings is a real possibility for the lower, hotter zones of the State where efficient placement of windows may not be adequate. Such arrangements use the heated air accumulated under the roof, through the stack or chimney effect, to create a suction or updraft which induces air movement and ventilation through the house even on still days. Figure 13 illustrates schematically the elements of such a system.

It should be noted that the riser stacks through which the warm air is vented are subject to some of the same aberrations as fireplace or heater chimneys. Localized winds or eddies may cause backdrafts. In such cases it may be necessary to top the stacks with rotary or directional vent caps. Tightly closing dampers or registers are necessary to seal off these systems in winter. If home-built, such dampers or closures should be made of seasoned wood or plywood and be carefully fitted. (The stacks and associated ductwork may generally be built of wood, as the air temperatures are not high enough to require metal.)

The air drawn into the house by such draft or venting effects should be from the coolest source possible, perhaps through windows on the northside wall. Special screened intake openings may be provided, opening at ground level at shady points amongst leafy plants and greenery. The principle may be carried still further and intake vents covered with evaporative-cooler matting kept moist by a trickle water supply. Because of the low draft heads or suction under which such non-powered systems operate, these vent openings must be comparatively large: on the order of not less than two or more square feet for the average room. This poses problems to the home builder in devising tight and well-insulated closures for them in winter. Few working examples of such systems exist from which to draw conclusions, and the whole field presents a good opportunity for experimentation by the resourceful

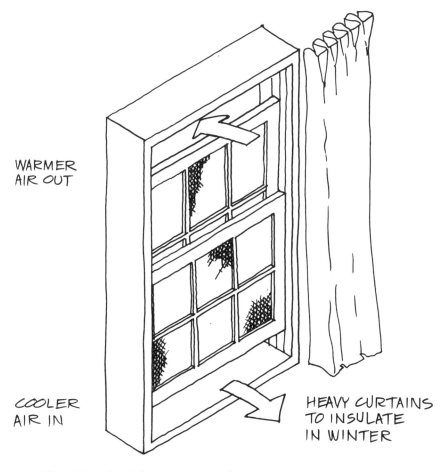

WARMER
AIR OUT

COOLER
AIR IN

HEAVY CURTAINS
TO INSULATE
IN WINTER

Fig. 12 Double Hung Window—Summer Ventilation

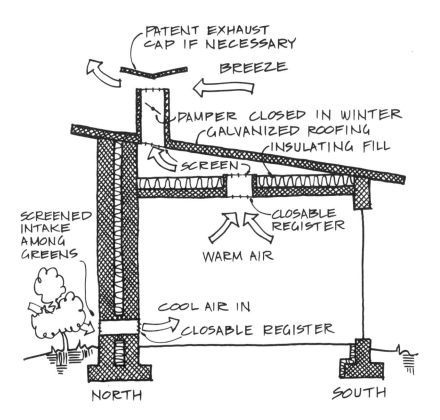

Fig. 13   Solar Ventilating—Schematic

energy-conserving home builder. Arrangements of this kind are probably not justified except in the hotter zones of the State, as a house built and ventilated in accordance with the principles outlined in preceding paragraphs will be comfortable in our uplands areas in all but the few unusually torrid summer days.

Siting and Landscaping for Climatic Tempering

NUMEROUS GOOD BOOKS have been written on the niceties of site planning and landscaping for the country, suburban, or town house, with a good deal of advice on how such siting and landscaping may contribute to the comfort, livability and energy conservation of the home, as well as to its esthetic appeal. The subject is a fascinating one, worthy of study in depth, and for those who wish to pursue it further some references are listed in the Bibliography. Only a few general comments may be attempted within the scope of this report. A first and most obvious one is that the time-honored custom of always facing a house parallel with street or road will have to be modified in many instances.

The orientation of a suntempered or solar house will clearly have to be determined more by the points of the compass than by the accidents of street or highway direction. (However, a variation of ten or even fifteen degrees from true south will not seriously affect the efficiency of the suntempering arrangement.) In a rural setting, with a tract of several or many acres on which to build, this does not present much of a problem, as the house may be situated at a suitable spot some distance back, and the layout of driveway and entrance approaches accommodated accordingly. On smaller tracts or suburban lots the adjustment may be more difficult. Here the internal plan of the house, with the resulting arrangement of volumes and surfaces on climatic principles, may be integrated with suitable placing of the entries and view windows such that convenient access between street, house and outdoor use areas is maintained.

A commonsense recommendation is for the use of deciduous (leaf-shedding) trees located for summer shade. The most critical location for this is the west exposure of the house which is subject to intense low-angle sunlight in summer afternoons and is apt to be a hotspot. Trees planted to shade this exposure in summer, but which become bare in winter and allow the solar warmth to reach the house then, can make a real contribution to the livability and energy-conserving qualities of the dwelling. If there is not room or time enough for trees, a similar effect can be achieved by trellis-climbing vines.

The advantages of locating on a south-facing slope, for winter weather modification, have been well known to country and rural home builders for centuries. This effect can be enhanced by digging the rear of the house into the hillside. If this is done the underground portion of the wall should be of masonry sufficiently massive or well reinforced to act as a retaining wall, and its outer surface should be waterproofed. It would also add to the thermal performance of the house if it were insulated from the earth mass by a barrier similar to the perimeter insulation previously discussed. Or the house may take advantage of the south slope by stepping up it, somewhat along the lines suggested in Figure 11. Lastly, if the slope is sufficiently steep, the house may be deliberately designed for a "convective rock storage" solar installation, with air collector panel located downhill from the house on the southern slope, or integral with the south stem wall. This is a somewhat more elaborate version of passive solar heating, and a design embodying it will be found in Appendix C.

Solar Energy for Food Production

ALONG WITH THE SHARP RISE in interest in solar heating and suntempering homes, there is a corresponding interest in the direct production of food through gardening, fruit and berry growing, poultry raising and small animal husbandry in connection with such homes. This is particularly characteristic of rural and village areas where, in any case, such subsistence agriculture and husbandry have been a part of the scene for generations. In view of ever-rising food and distribution costs, both in terms of money and of energy, this is a trend worth encouraging. We have not attempted a dissertation on the most efficient layout of garden, orchard trees, animal and poultry runs, sheds, etc.—and again, there is an excellent and growing literature on the subject. (See Bibliography.) However, attempt has been consistently made throughout this study to work out suggested house plans which are adapted to this way of life and activity. It seems an unfortunate fact that most country homes now being designed and built are not, in fact, country homes in this sense, since their kitchens, equipment, and food storage arrangements are identical with those of typical town or suburban homes and are laid out mainly to conveniently utilize supermarket frozen, packaged or canned foods.

Any arrangements to handle more basic food preparation and storage requirements are usually afterthoughts and improvisations or imperfect holdovers of traditional methods. It is now possible and desirable to begin designing homes which are fitted to modern ideas of comfort, convenience and lifestyle, yet which can efficiently provide for many of the life-supporting and self-provisioning activities which have been carried on in most households since time immemorial.

The most popular and visible of these new-era dwelling modifications is the attached or lean-to greenhouse already briefly discussed. These differ from the traditional conservatory or hothouse in that they do not require artificial heat at night or in wintertime, but actually contribute substantially to the heating needs of the house to which they are attached. This is accomplished by: (a) venting the excess warm air trapped during the sunshine hours on even chilly winter days into the main body of the house; (b) cutting down the proportion of glazed sky-facing surface in the layout of the greenhouse and providing a measure of opaque and insulated overhang to prevent excessive heat loss by radiation to the cold night sky; and (c) double-glazing the transparent surfaces and providing insulating shutters or closures in unusually cold locations. A partial sinking of the greenhouse into the earth also increases the temperature stability of the installation (formerly called the pit greenhouse, now popularly called the growhole). Designs in Appendix C show possible versions of such installations in a suntempered house. The Solar Sustenance Project, a companion Four Corners funded research and demonstration program to this one, gives much information on the design and construction of greenhouses in north central New Mexico and the productivity which may be expected of them if they are well managed. See Bibliography.

The small greenhouse is primarily a device for providing a modest but continuous supply of vitamin-rich salads and mainly leafy vegetables throughout most of the year, without benefit of migrant labor agribusiness, long-distance hauling and mass merchandising. In a well-functioning subsistence or productive homestead, however, a large measure of essential foodstuffs—fruits, tubers, legumes, cereals, poultry, milk products, fish and red meat—may be produced and harvested from the surrounding land mainly in the summer and fall and must be prepared and stored for year-round use.

Perhaps the first house design element to make this whole process more convenient and manageable is what has been called variously the harvest, summer or preserving kitchen— a facility which has been characteristic of working farm or country homes in many parts of the country until a generation or two ago. This is essentially a working space with convenient access to garden, orchard, etc., and which is equipped with counters or tables, a cutting block, a sink for rough scrubbing of produce and a generous cooking range (often wood burning) for operations such as scalding, blanching or glass-jar canning. Waste water from the scrubbing sink may be piped out to garden or orchard directly since it contains no fecal matter. (Oils and fats should be excluded from this waste.) The compost pit or bin may also be placed conveniently to receive parings and trimmings. Since this space will be used primarily in summer and fall, its heating arrangements may be minimal, and it should probably be located on the north side of the house. In New Mexico it may be virtually out of doors in the form of a working patio, where the *horno* or adobe beehive baking oven may be located. (This also often turns out to be an *al fresco* social center.) Other outdoor food-processing equipment might include a small smoke house, a solar dehydrator (see Appendix D) or fruit and vegetable drier, and a hoisting frame for butchering large animal carcasses.

It would seem logical to include laundry equipment in the indoor harvest kitchen space. This may consist simply of laundry trays or may include a washing machine—preferably, from the point of view of low cost and energy conservation, one of the simple gravity-draining type. The question of gas or electric clothes driers will have to be left to individual discretion. These are highly consumptive of commercial energy and their use will become increasingly costly as rates go up. Even if installed, it would be good strategy to plan a set of clothes lines (solar clothes driers!) conveniently located to the laundry exit. If placed along a high south-facing garden wall the utility of such drying lines would be increased, especially in winter, due to the reflection of sunlight and infrared heat from the wall. If the harvest kitchen also doubles as laundry in this fashion, its plumbing should be laid out for easy draining in winter to prevent freezing. An inexpensive wood burning chunk stove could be provided to warm up the space when it is in actual use so that the heating system of the main house need not be taxed for this purpose.

The harvest kitchen should obviously be planned for convenient access to ample storage facilities. The lowest costing and least energy-consumptive of such facilities is some version of the traditional *subterraneo* or root cellar. Through good design this may be incorporated in the main body of the house at the same level as or only slightly lower than the general floor level. It should contain ample shelving for the cool storage of canned, smoked or pickled foods, bins for apples and potatoes, etc. This *subterraneo* and its access door should be carefully constructed and tightly fitted to keep out mice and rats and other small creatures of the countryside. A pantry with abundant shelf space for the storage of less temperature-sensitive foods and for such items as preserving jars could form a transitional space between the harvest kitchen and the more conventional modern kitchen in which the daily meals are prepared.

It is suggested that wherever firewood is accessible and commonly used, even this modern kitchen be equipped with a good wood burning range in addition to the customary gas unit. An electric range is currently the choice of many, but it must be pointed out that in terms of overall efficiency, taking into account power plant and transmission losses, electricity for cooking, heating and water heating is very wasteful and its use for these purposes in the future will become increasingly costly and undesirable. The same comment applies to the electric deep freezer which, together with the large refrigerator, is a major user of domestic electricity. Space in the harvest kitchen or pantry could be allotted to a conventional freezer, preferably of the top-opening chest type, but the prudent householder will not allow it to displace the several other methods of food preservation which are thoroughly satisfactory and which are not dependent on high commercial energy inputs and on complicated technology.

Several of the schematic house designs presented in Appendix C suggest some of the arrangements of these various working spaces in relation to the main suntempered house plan. It must be emphasized that these designs are suggestive only, as requirements vary greatly from family to family and many householders have strong opinions as to the desirable kitchen and work space layout. Also the actual equipment installed will vary greatly according to the dietary habits of the family and the ambitiousness of its food production program. Obviously such processes as cheese-, butter- and wine-making will require special equipment and perhaps special work spaces to be carried out efficiently.

Hot water for kitchen, harvest kitchen and laundry (as well as for bathrooms) should be provided to as large an extent as possible by one or more solar water heaters. The general placement of the collector panels and tanks for these heaters is shown in the various schematic plans. The output of these solar units may be backed up by heat exchangers in the flues or fireboxes of wood heating stoves or even fireplaces,* or they may be backed up by conventional butane water heaters (which, however, will consume considerably less fuel than normal, since the water fed to them will be at least preheated by the solar units).

---

*See descriptive text for van Dresser house, Appendix C.

Backing-up the Suntempering System

PRACTICAL EXPERIENCE AS well as theoretical studies indicate that complete comfort level solar heating of a New Mexico dwelling under all conditions is not usually feasible despite the theoretical surplus of solar energy during the winter. (There are one or two experimenters who report 100% solar heating in their habitats, but this is achieved by systems and methods of construction and insulation which are prohibitively demanding for the average moderate-to-low income home builder.) The practical percentage of solar heating for the entire heating season, as mentioned before, varies from 50% to 80%, with the average reported in the range of 65-70%. The deficiency may show up in the form of slightly subcomfort temperatures over prolonged periods, or shorter periods of temperatures in the low 50s or even lower in extreme weather. For such periods fuel-generated back-up heating must obviously be provided (although again the amount of such back-up will vary greatly according to the habits and temperament of the house dwellers).

If this back-up is conventional heating apparatus—most likely either butane- or gas-fired room space heaters or a central forced warm-air furnace—for a well-insulated and tightly built suntempered house along the lines so far discussed, it would probably be safe to size the heating units about one-third smaller than would be standard practice for a conventional residence of the same floor area. The actual fuel consumption by this system might be substantially less than one-third below normal, depending on the quality of the house design and construction, the accidents of the season and the management skill of the occupants. But sufficient capacity should be provided to handle unusually cold and cloudy periods. The safety factor may vary for different areas of the house: those in constant sedentary use (e.g., living room or study) require a higher temperature for comfort than those devoted to active or infrequent usage.

The same general comments apply to electric back-up heating with the additional reservation that this is an inherently wasteful way of utilizing the energy of primary fuel (coal, oil or gas burned at the power plant). Furthermore, power companies whose technicians usually design and size electric heating installations have generally not gotten around to recognizing the effectiveness of suntempering methods and, hence, will make no allowance for them in their engineering. Finally, their rate structures penalize the use of electricity in moderate quantities for auxiliary purposes. These are factors which may be modified in the next few years, but the inherent high cost of electricity for general heating and the problem of meeting peak load demands economically are not likely to alter.*

For many parts of rural and non-urban New Mexico, firewood remains a practical and economic source of back-up heating energy. (In this connection, it is interesting to note that only with the year 1976 did the energy produced by nuclear power in the United States as a whole equal that produced by firewood.) In 1975 the combined officially reported firewood gathered from all of New Mexico's five national forests was about 63,400 cords.** The potential heat energy in this much wood amounts to about 16 million therms, or enough to heat about 20,000 of our typical 1,800 square foot houses in the Santa Fe climatic zone. Allowing for the working efficiency of most wood burners, this figure should probably be cut in half. However, the quantity of wood reported is probably consider-

---

*The heat pump, a thermal-mechanical machine for concentrating low-temperature warmth into higher-temperature heat, uses electricity several times more efficiently than ordinary resistance heaters. It is a relatively expensive industrially produced device.

**Special compilation by the Technology Application Center, University of New Mexico.

ably below that actually gathered and no allowance is made for the large quantities of waste wood consumed for no useful purpose in the slab burners of the various regional sawmills.

If all the houses utilizing this forest output for auxiliary heat were suntempered, well-insulated and equipped with wood burners of maximum efficiency, the total number could well be in the range of 40,000 or more. Bearing in mind that the fuel supplied in this fashion is essentially waste, scrap and forest thinnings and, if properly managed, does not harm the sustained yield management of our forests, it is obvious that this is an important potential in the overall energy budget of the State and the economic well-being of many of its inhabitants. It might also be pointed out that in the average family wood-gathering operation, the B.T.U.s per load of wood gathered probably is at least 10 times greater than the B.T.U. value of the gasoline expended for the purpose. This compares not unfavorably with the extraction and distribution costs in energy for most commercial fuels. It further follows that the villages and towns of the rural uplands regions situated close to wooded and forested lands have a particular advantage in this energy-conserving respect. The economic development and redevelopment policies of the State should take this into account as an alternative to the unlimited growth of a few larger cities and their suburbs. These entities are notoriously energy-consuming.

As to the specific means by which wood heat is utilized in the home, some general comments are warranted here:

(1) Wood burning heaters, particularly some of the modern thermostatically controlled types, are substantially more efficient than even the best fireplaces. Where wood is seriously depended on for consistent and prolonged supplementary heat rather than for occasional room tempering, such stoves should be used.

(2) They should be located centrally in the rooms or spaces they are intended to heat, not pocketed in corners. Bear in mind that a good proportion of their heat energy is given off in the form of infrared rays which can be picked up and stored in adjacent walls, just as solar heat is stored. For this purpose the same type of massive walls previously discussed, externally insulated where exposed to the outside, are desirable.

(3) The large conventional British-type fireplace should

be avoided, despite its sentimental attraction. Such a fireplace ("big enough to roast a steer in") is a glutton for logs, and a large percentage of the heat it produces goes up the chimney. However, the small traditional New Mexican arched fireplace may be used to good effect and for occasional chilly evenings. It may be built cheaply, mostly of native materials, and if properly designed can be quite efficient. The "shepherd's fireplace" is a variant of this type. It is proportioned to maximize the area of hot firebox surface radiating outward into the room.

Other variants are circulating fireplaces (with fireboxes jacketed in metal so that they act as miniature hot-air furnaces), various versions of the Franklin stove and the free-standing circular fireplace with metal hood. All fireplaces should be equipped with closable dampers to cut down heat loss when not in use. There is a considerable range of opinion as to the relative excellence of these various types, and not much scientific data on which to base judgment. A consensus seems to be forming, however, that it is worth installing a special duct to bring outside air to the firebox of most fireplaces. This provides the essential combustion air without drawing on the already warmed air of the room and wasting it up the chimney. There are a number of good manuals on this subject. (See Bibliography.)

(4) There is room for improvement in the layout of houses in which wood is the prime source of auxiliary heat. Covered firewood storage should be provided with convenient access to the principal wood burning devices. (Oddly enough this simple arrangement is not usually found even in old farmhouses of the region.) These storage spaces should also be convenient to truck delivery of firewood if it is purchased already cut and split, or to some sort of outdoor work space in which logs or slabs may be stockpiled, sawn and split as needed.

A more thoroughgoing design adaptation to efficient wood heating is through the use of one central warm air furnace from which heat is led to the various parts of the house through ducts. A generation or two ago this was common practice and warm air furnaces installed in cellars from which the heated air could rise by convection were standard units. Such furnaces have completely disappeared from the market, but it is possible that the present revival of interest in locally available fuels will bring them back in more modern and efficient forms. Appendix C shows a house design for a partial adaptation of this principle, using a large wood space-heating stove as a central unit with supply and return ducts to distribute the heat throughout the house.

It should also be mentioned that most of the preceding comments apply also to the use of locally mined coal. There are a fair number of mines scattered throughout the State which have continued to be worked in a small way and it is possible that the energy crunch will make such operations more financially feasible. Here again such alternative energy development would be greatly aided by the availability of domestic-sized but efficient coal-burning furnaces and cooking ranges designed for clean combustion and the minimal emission of smoke. Used in suntempered and energy-conserving houses, the actual amount of coal such units would require could be quite low, thus justifying the higher costs of mining and transporting under present and near-future economic conditions. (The famous AGA cooking range invented in Sweden by a Nobel prize-winning physicist is said to maintain full baking and cooking heat for 24 hours on one bucketful of coal.) It is to be hoped that New Mexican inventors, manufacturers and development authorities will combine to explore such possibilities.

A more exotic source of fuel—methane gas generated by the decomposition of organic wastes—is now much discussed by the advocates of alternative energy development. The best future for this technique appears to be at the community, town or small city scale, where sizable amounts of a variety of organic wastes can be collected and processed in a plant with a fair degree of technical sophistication and scientific management. Good sized stock-raising or dairy farms may also support such a process, where large quantities of animal manure are regularly available. In fact, methane generators were in extensive use on French hog farms in the 1940s, according to a pamphlet published by the French Forestries Service.* Well documented examples of continuously successful applications

---

Gaz de Fumier a la Ferme, by F. Mignotte, La Maison Rustique, Paris, Librairie Agricole, Horticole, Forestiere et Menagere, 26 Rue Jacob.

by individual householders using only the wastes from the household are, however, virtually non-existent. Here again it is to be hoped that research and pilot development of community-sized methane plants will be vigorously pursued in New Mexico, particularly in situations where the fertilizer byproduct can effectively be applied in intensive farming and market gardening.*

---

*The Four Corners Regional Commission has contracted with the Colorado Energy Research Institute for small-scale demonstrations for methane gas generation utilizing agricultural wastes and is currently negotiating a contract for the design and engineering for large-scale commercial production of methane gas utilizing agricultural waste.

Solar Water Heating

THE DIRECT USE OF THE sun's radiant energy for the heating of water is probably the most successful and widespread technique in the field, dating back to the 1920s in southern Florida and California and having very considerable application in countries such as Australia, Israel and Japan. Before World War II the technology of simple domestic solar water heaters was standardized in Florida and a recent pamphlet well summarizes this technology.*

Despite this history of achievement, it cannot be said that a time-proven, low-to-moderate-cost solar water heating unit which can be recommended to New Mexico home builders exists either as a manufactured package product or as a standardized do-it-yourself kit or set of instructions. There are several reasons for this. The most obvious is that in New Mexico we have to reckon with below-freezing nights a good part of the year, even though daytime sunshine is usually sufficient for water heating. A system which works well in climates where freezing temperatures occur rarely or not at all cannot be simply transplanted here, as the large exposed area of water-filled tubes or channels which make up the typical collector panel will probably be ruptured on the first freezing night. Solutions exist for this problem, but thanks to the orgy of superscale pe-

---

*Published by the Environmental Center of the Florida Conservation Foundation, Inc., 935 Orange Avenue, Suite E, Winter Park, Florida 32789. *How to Build a Solar Water Heater*, prepared for the Florida Energy Committee, 24 pp., June 1975, $3.50.

troleum exploitation which followed World War II, the techniques necessary were not worked on seriously. It is only quite recently that this situation is beginning to improve, but the state of the art is in process of change, and we are still awaiting practical, widely applicable systems—which indeed may well be different from region to region and for different economic and lifestyle conditions.

The problem is further complicated by skyrocketing prices of the main materials used in the original systems—copper sheet and copper tubing, which are now almost prohibitive. Still another complication is the enormously increased scale and centralization of manufacturing. Specialty items for solar water heaters—such as storage tanks, collector panels and heat exchangers—formerly could be produced at relatively small scale and reasonable cost in local or regional metal fabricating establishments. They are now almost unobtainable unless ordered in very large quantities, or unless custom-made at extremely high prices. (Incidentally, the same difficulties apply to the production of other energy-saving devices such as wind pumps, wind generators, bicycles and woodstoves which, if manufactured at all, cost many times more than they used to.)

This does not mean that successful solar water heaters cannot be built in New Mexico. A considerable number have been and are being installed, but they tend to be either the result of individual ingenuity and resourcefulness in the use of available or salvage materials, or expensive units assembled from manufactured elements.

At this point it will be helpful to look at the kinds of systems which are beginning to be worked out as a result of many diversified efforts.

By far the most common is one version or another of the classic Florida-style heater already mentioned. (See Figure 14.) This system consists of an elevated and heavily insulated storage tank, usually of 80 to 100 gallons capacity, connected through riser and return pipes to a tilted solar collection panel below it. This panel, essentially a shallow glass-covered box containing a zigzag or grid of black-painted pipe soldered to a black-painted metal backing, is—during sunny periods—a source of heated water which rises to the upper part of the tank by natural convection and gradually fills it in the course of the solar day, while the cooler water at the bottom drops down to the panel to be heated in its turn. Under strong sunlight the water so heated may frequently reach 160°F. or even higher, if the various parts of the system are correctly proportioned. Often the collector panel is installed on the south slope of a gabled roof with the tank in the peak of the attic or if necessary in a false chimney or turret. Water in the whole system is maintained under city pressure and is withdrawn from the top of the tank as needed, just as in a conventional gas or electric water heater.

This system is modified for service in a climate with periodic freezing temperatures by filling the collector panel and the riser and return pipes with antifreeze solution rather than water. This part of the system is no longer connected directly into the storage tank but to a heat exchanger (most commonly

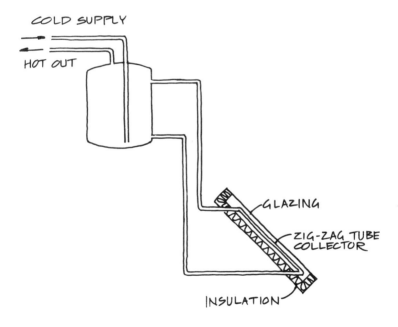

Fig. 14   Solar Water Heater for Non-freezing Climate

a jacket around the tank) which allows the hot antifreeze to heat the water inside the tank without mixing with it. (See Figure 15.) The physical principles governing this system are easily understood and a few fairly simple rules-of-thumb are a useful guide for building and installing it. Some of these are: the area of collector panel should be roughly one square foot for each gallon of storage capacity. It should face within ten degrees or so of due south, and its tilt should be roughly equal to the latitude of its location (around 36 degrees in northern New Mexico). The riser and return pipes should slope as uniformly as possible upward to the tank, with no dips in which air pockets may form to stop the natural circulation of the antifreeze. The bottom of the tank should be not less than 2 or 3 feet higher than the top of the panel. The antifreeze circuit

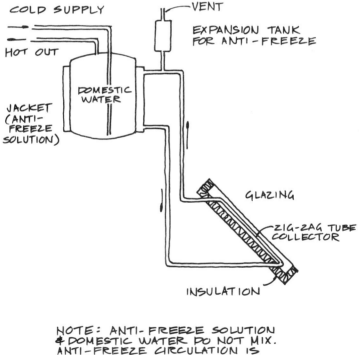

Fig. 15 Solar Water Heater for Freezing Climate

should be vented at its highest point to allow escape of air bubbles and there should be excess capacity above the hot inlet to the heat exchanger jacket, to allow for expansion and contraction and for the gradual loss of solution. As in any water heater, the hot feed to the house should be connected to the top of the tank and the cold supply to the tank introduced through a drop-pipe which leads down to within a few inches of the bottom. The tank and antifreeze hot riser should, of course, be well insulated.

There is little in question about these general principles. The main challenges to present-day builders and installers of such systems are: how and of what materials may an efficient and long-lasting collector panel be built or acquired at reasonable cost? Where can one obtain a pressure-tight, corrosion-proof storage tank of the right dimensions and with the necessary connection fittings for solar use? What sort of heat exchanger can be fitted to this tank to give efficient leak-proof long-term service for a moderate investment? How best may the entire system be designed into a house to avoid excessively long pipe runs and awkward "plumber's nightmares," while still providing convenient access for maintenance?

Responses to these various questions are still individualized and quite varied. There are no prepackaged or widely accepted solutions. This is to be expected. The state of the art is about comparable to that of the automobile industry in 1910. But techniques, products and practical know-how are gradually evolving. Several manufactured collector panels are on the market (although the prices, bottoming at about $8 per square foot, exclusive of shipping costs from eastern points or foreign nations, are not encouraging to the moderate-income home builder). Resourceful inventors and experimenters are building their own panels out of galvanized sheet or corrugated iron roofing, aluminum, or copper sheets and tubing (despite its expense), cast concrete, and even plastic pipe which will not rupture when frozen. The collector panel has been bypassed entirely by heating water through a heat exchanger placed in the path of the warm air from the main house-heating panel, or by enclosing the storage tank itself in a reflecting shell exposed to sunlight by day and closed by heavily insulated hatches at night. Storage tanks are devised of salvaged gas water heaters or pressure tanks. For the present the energy-conserving home builder must depend in this field on his own knowledge of basic physics, his craftsmanship and resourcefulness, or must find someone with these qualities who has already acquired some practical know-how. Fortunately this situation is rapidly improving and, within a decade, knowledge of the subject will be widely diffused and products and practitioners of the art will be much more available. In the meantime it may be stated that solar water heating is a natural for New Mexico and is well worth the attention of pioneers in the movement towards resources conservation and non-exploitive living techniques.

The Special Genius of New Mexico

THOSE WHO HAVE READ THROUGH this book to this point will have discovered for themselves that it is not a detailed, step-by-step how-to-do-it manual or building trades handbook. This is not accidental. There are a number of such works on the market and available at bookstores and libraries, which go at considerable length into the details of adobe-making and laying, the placing of footings, the setting of window and door frames and lintels, the framing of roofs, the installation of sanitary and supply piping, and so on. An attempt has been made to list several of these references—a number of which have been published specifically in and for New Mexico—in the Bibliography.

Over and above this generally accessible "book learning," however, there is—especially in rural and traditional New Mexico—an unusually widespread working familiarity with the realities of home construction using native materials at hand. There are many communities within which the building of a house is still very much a family affair, with several generations participating in the mixing and laying of adobe, the hauling in, barking and placing of *vigas*, and all the other steps in creating a habitation literally from the ground up. And this familiarity is being generously shared with new settlers in the region, many of whom have become skilled craftsmen and small building contractors in their own right.

This is an ideal situation for the nurturing and diffusion of an effective latter-day folk technology in solar utilization. As indicated in our opening remarks, its grassroots practitioners have already pioneered valuable pilot experiments in the field and, as a result, New Mexico now has an international reputation for this type of pioneering.

Government policies, it is hoped, will be designed to facilitate and reinforce this trend. Research funds should be allotted as much to small-scale low technology projects as to impressive corporate or institutionally sponsored—and highly expensive—advanced projects. Building and zoning codes should be carefully thought out to encourage intelligent use of low-cost indigenous material, and sufficient vocational training programs should be directed to the same ends.

A small but promising start has been made in the current New Mexico legislative provision for a tax rebate on solar elements in home construction. It is important that this law be interpreted to include elements of simple passive systems, and not only factory-made components.

Considering the circumstances, it was felt most useful to direct this book towards this widespread body of independent artisans and owner-builders in the State. For such readers a general survey and getting together of known basic principles of suntempering and climatic design would be of interest, while over-specific presentation of construction details would be unnecessary and perhaps even presumptuous, would result in a cluttered text and conceivably get in the way of the sort of creative and innovative application of basic principles which leads to progress. For those starting from scratch, and wishing to be filled in on the ABCs of practical building, there are the references already cited, and also the most valuable resource of the advice and example of knowledgeable neighbors. The State is also fortunate in having one of the largest and most active regional solar organizations in the world—the New Mexico Solar Energy Association—which maintains information and demonstration programs.

In short, the stage is set in New Mexico for a breakthrough in the effective development of a true non-exploitive, ecologically adapted economy and lifestyle at the grassroots level. We may sincerely hope that the *special genius of New Mexico* will make a unique contribution to the solution of looming national and worldwide problems in the coming decades.

Appendices

APPENDIX A

BUDGET

Allocations provided by the Four Corners Regional Commission to the Sundwellings team over a two-year period:

Category	Allocation
Design	$ 4,000
Reproduction and Printing	2,000
Technical Review Team	10,600
Project Coordinator	9,200
Secretarial and Bookkeeping	1,000
Travel Expenses	1,000
Ghost Ranch Administrative	1,500
Demonstration Materials	4,700
	$34,000

APPENDIX B

CONTENTS OF PROGRESS REPORTS

Individual papers listed below may be obtained from the Four Corners Regional Commission, Suite 238, Petroleum Building, 3535 E. 30th Street, Farmington, N.M. 87401.

It is to be remembered that the art of solar heating is still in the exploratory stage. These papers are preliminary studies and must be treated accordingly.

---

*Designs are all preliminary and are not for general release, but may be inspected at office of Four Corners Regional Commission and at the New Mexico Solar Energy Association, mailing address P. O. Box 2004, Santa Fe, N. M. 87501.

APPENDIX C

SUNDWELLINGS DESIGNS

Expandable Prototype House

The following schematic designs are not intended to be working drawings but are included to suggest how a simple suntempered home of adobe might be laid out for the home or self-help builder. The house is designed to be expandable from a minimal unit of a living room, kitchen and bath (Figure C1) to a four-bedroom house with study or shop, 1½ baths, cool-storage room, pantry and summer kitchen (Figure C4). All the versions of this house may be built with or without the south-facing greenhouse, although the greenhouse version will probably perform better thermally and will generally be desired by the home builder as offering special side benefits.

Figure C1 shows the initial minimal unit—a simple rectangular structure 28' x 35' with a gabled roof. It is constructed of 14" thick adobe walls with ceiling of local lumber supported on *vigas* (peeled logs). Over this ceiling is an ordinary gabled roof formed of rough lumber and roofed with either galvanized iron or 90 lb. slate coat. On top of the ceiling is a 10" layer of any type of available insulation—perlite, coarse sawdust, 6" of glass wool, etc. The north wall of this unit is shown with temporary furring filled with the same insulation to shield against the cold northern exposure. Later this wall will become an interior wall and then the temporary furring can be removed and the lumber used elsewhere in the building.

The west wall may also be treated in the same fashion if expansion is contemplated; otherwise this may be a double wall filled with pumice. The space under the north portion of this unit is shown as an open *portal* for the storage of tools, firewood, and the many other necessaries which must be kept under shelter during the pioneering phase of the occupancy.

The south wall of this unit will consist either of large direct gain windows or such windows alternating with sections of Trombe wall, as described in the text. If a greenhouse is built or contemplated, openable sash must be provided at the top and bottom of these windows to allow free circulation of warm air from the greenhouse into the main building and return cool air circulation at the floor level. This return circulation may be made more efficient by the provision of one or more ducts under the floor, leading from the rear of the room to the base of the greenhouse (Figures C8 to C10). They may be simply made of treated lumber, salvaged culvert, etc., but should be at least a square foot in cross section. In either case, openable windows in portions of the south exposure are essential.

Suggested low-cost native material floors are: adobe hardened with linseed oil, bitumen or one of the new plastic base sealers; flagstone laid in adobe and pointed with cement mortar; or brick laid in sand. In all cases perimeter insulation should be provided (see cross section figures and main text).

Figure C2 shows the next phase of expansion of this unit. The northern *portal* space is now utilized for a small bedroom or study, pantry, a cool-storage room and a small wood-storage *portal*. Interior insulation is provided on the inner south wall of this room to guard against inflow of warmth from the main house into this area.

Figure C3 shows two more bedrooms added to the west side of the house. The small initial bedroom may be maintained as such or converted to a workshop or utility room, according to the needs of the family. A summer kitchen is shown added to the east facade. This may or may not be desired, depending on the extensiveness of the food preparation of the family.

A small sheltered overhang is provided at the rear of the newly added bedroom for firewood storage. Firewood from this supply may be carried into the house through a door into the study or shop. A small modern wood heater is suggested in the northeast corner of the living room.

Figure C4 shows the final expansion of the design into a four-bedroom home. A half bath is added between the two westernmost bedrooms. The summer or harvest kitchen is not shown in this particular design but could be added with no complications. The greenhouse is shown running the full length of this structure but, if desired, it could be stopped short of the two westernmost bedrooms and direct gain or Trombe wall substituted for the south exposure here. However, the greenhouse would shade this facade in the morning hours and would probably somewhat lower the efficiency of the solar function.

Figure C5 shows a typical cross section through the bathroom sector of all versions of this house. It also shows schematically the mounting of the solar water heater panel and tank. The exact location of this element would depend on the wishes and pocketbook of the builder. If the expected consumption of hot water is low, a single collector and tank roughly centered over the bath-hall room area might be adequate, although it will require fairly long runs to carry the hot water to the kitchen from the storage tank. In this case the tank and collector should be relatively large—probably not less than 80 gallons capacity —and with 80 square feet of collector surface. The general principle governing such installation is described in the text and the Bibliography contains specific reference material on the components of such systems.

Alternatively, two smaller tanks and collectors might be placed, one over the bathroom area and one over the kitchen area. It might be desirable to connect these solar tanks to small capacity gas or electric water heaters in the kitchen and bathroom if an absolutely reliable source of hot water is desired and is financially possible for the builder.

Another alternative would be to install a heat exchanger in conjunction with the flue of the kitchen wood range to provide a supplementary source of hot water.

Figure C6 is a section through the westernmost bedrooms of the largest version of the house. This shows a break in the roof necessary to provide the slight additional depth for the additional bedrooms and half bath at this end of the house.

Figure C7 suggests a means of capturing additional solar warmth for any of the rear bedrooms of the house. Air heated within the attic space is sucked down through a simple duct leading into the desired bedroom. A low-wattage blower or fan is necessary in this portion of the system. It might be controlled thermostatically or even manually. Cool air, in return, is sucked into a duct at the north end of the room and is conducted to the south lower corner of the attic space. These ducts may be very simply made of 1x10 lumber and, where they run down interior walls, could harmonize with the general style of the house. To increase the effectiveness of this sytem (which has come to be called the "Florence flow system" by the Design team, since the author's wife thought of it while working in the hot attic of our tin-roofed, 200-year-old adobe house on a freezing but sunny winter's day), an interior partition is carried up inside the attic to seal off the colder northern portion of the attic.

Figure C8 shows a flat-roofed variation of the general plan for those who prefer the pueblo silhouette and can handle the necessary built-up roofing for the flat area. In this design the rear bedrooms are heated by clerestory windows, double-glazed, with closable shutters for night insulation.

Figure C9 shows a simple lean-to greenhouse applied to the gabled-roof version of the design. Note that the greenhouse is excavated slightly below the interior floor level. This allows greater south-facing area and also provides some stabilization of temperature by the surrounding earth.

Figure C10 shows a more ambitious greenhouse with vertical south wall. The sloping roof provided by this greenhouse allows a lower mounting for one or more water heater panels, thus permitting the installation of a larger tank in the attic space, while still keeping the bottom of this tank above the top of the collector panel. This figure also shows the corner fireplace in the living room with its chimney tall enough to clear eddy currents from the roof ridge.

Figure C11 shows a convection circulation underfloor rock storage system suitable for a site with a definite southward slope. A layer of smooth uniform fist-sized rocks is provided under the floor from 18-24" deep. Heated air from a collector panel is conducted across the top of this bed through an air space; thence filters down through the bed as it cools, and returns to the lower edge of the collector panel. In this case the floor may be formed by laying new or good salvaged corrugated roofing on spacer bricks, then filling with sand or earth carrying brick, flagstone, or hardened adobe, as suggested previously. The mass of this floor will provide part of the storage system and will gently and uniformly radiate warmth into the room above. The return air space under the rock bed may be formed by laying coarse mesh, again on spacer bricks. The mesh should be capable of supporting the weight of the rocks above.

Figure C11 also sketches a warm air-venting system as discussed in the text and installed in the Ghost Ranch test/demonstration buildings. A large chimney-like stack (which may be made of wood) is built in the roof adjacent to the ridge. Small-

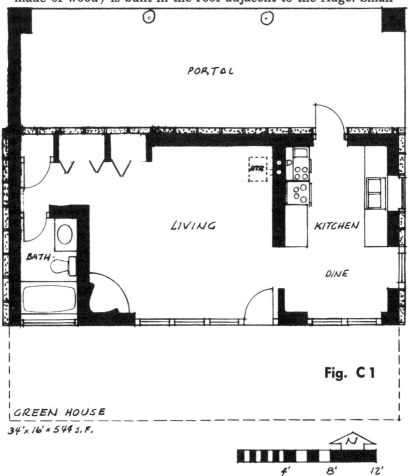

Fig. C 1

GREEN HOUSE

34' x 16' = 544 S.F.

er vents, not less than one foot square, are built in the ceilings of the various rooms, communicating with the attic space. These vents and the upper stack are closed during the heating season. Several such stacks could be built, depending on the size of the house. Each large stack should be no less than 4 square feet in cross section. (See Appendix E.)

Figure C12 shows a different version of the subfloor system with the collector panel placed vertically on the southern stem wall. This convective storage system might be used for only a portion of the house and can be used in conjunction with direct gain, Trombe wall or Florence-flow supplementary solar heat.

It should be emphasized that these plans are not working drawings. They assume a knowledge of practical regional construction techniques or the ability to acquire them and also they assume that the builder has absorbed and will apply the principles set forth in the main body of this book.

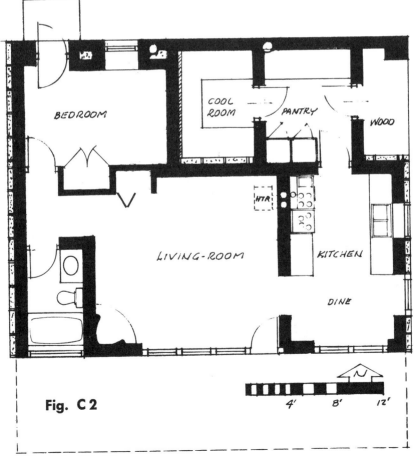

Fig. C 2

4'   8'   12'

34'x 26.5' = 901. S.F.

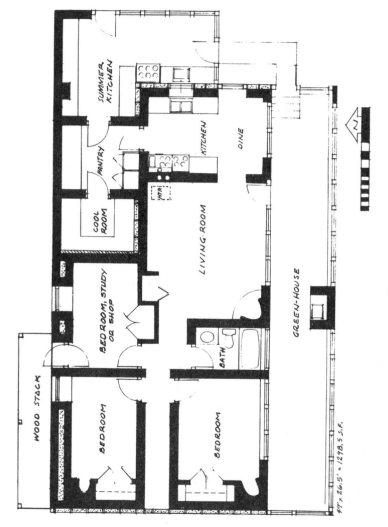

Fig. C 3

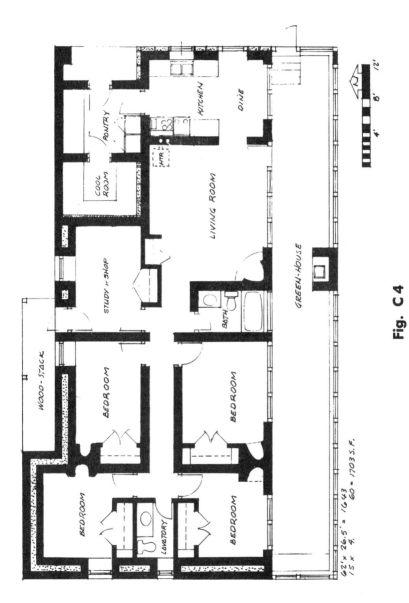

Fig. C 4

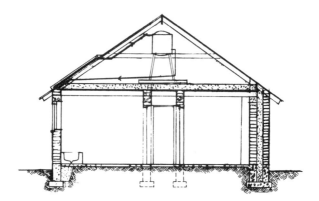

Fig. C 5

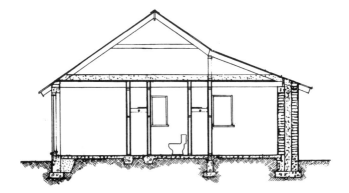

Fig. C 6

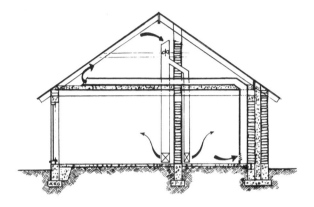

Fig. C 7

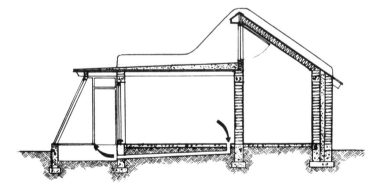

Fig. C 8

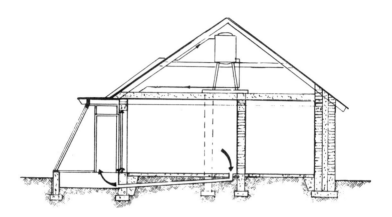

Fig. C 9

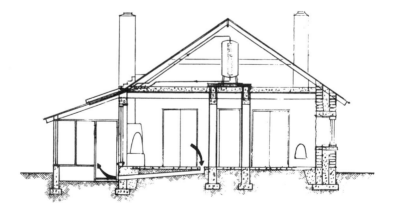

Fig. C 10

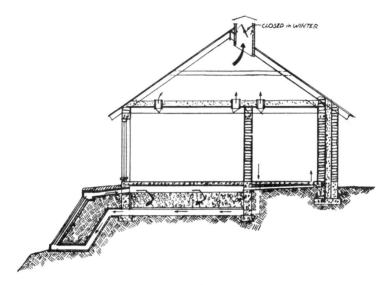

Fig. C 11

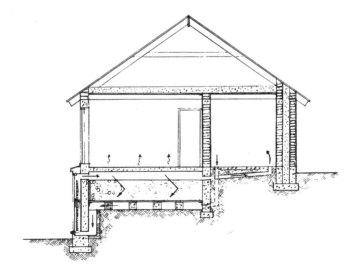

Fig. C 12

van Dresser House, El Rito

The main characteristic of this design is the use of virtually the entire roof area as an unglazed solar air-heating panel. Although it is well known that an unglazed panel is considerably less efficient than its glazed equivalent, this disadvantage may be more than compensated for by the very large available area and the low cost of the construction. The roof will be required in any case, and relatively slight modifications in its design will enable it to serve as a collector panel. The requirements of this design dictated a south-sloping single rake or shed roof to give maximum exposure to the low winter sun (Figure C13). The material selected for the roof covering is ordinary galvanized corrugated iron roofing, as this material, especially when weathered, has very good absorbing characteristics and, to some extent, inhibits the reradiation of infrared heat. The air collecting feature of the roof is provided by spacing this corrugated roofing about 1¼" above the regular roof sheathing (Figure C14), thus providing a laminar space in which hot air can accumulate and rise toward a high north eave of the house. Along this eave a collecting duct is provided with several down ducts leading to a rock storage pit under the north corridor of the house. In these ducts small low-wattage blowers or axial-flow fans provide the necessary down draft. This pit is fairly conventional in design with clean fist-sized rocks and provision for the air to enter it at several points for even distribution through the bed. After passing through the bed, the air is released into the north corridor through vents along the base of the wall and thence makes its way to intake vents at the south end of each room and is drawn up to the lower edge of the roof panel where it is reheated and recirculated.

Beneath the air flow space forming the upper layer of the roof, there is a complete second roof 8" thick filled with sawdust for inexpensive but effective insulation, and supported on 3x8" transverse rafters. This roof, therefore, is not to be confused with a skylight or greenhouse-type roof. It is very effectively insulated from heat loss to the night sky and the heat gathered during the day is stored in the interior of the house. From below the roof looks like the traditional northern New Mexican ceiling using native lumber which may be rough-planed and stained and rough-sawn rafters. *Vigas* could equally be substituted for the sawn rafters.

The south sloping roof necessarily lowers the south facade so that large high direct gain windows or Trombe walls are not feasible with this design. However, a half-height waterwall extends for the full length of the south facade and forms an auxiliary solar heat receptor and heat storage bank containing some forty 17 gallon army surplus containers for direct absorption and storage of heat (Figure C15). This waterwall may be closed at night by hinged light-colored panels which, when down, reflect additional sunlight into the heat accumulator bank. The space above this heat bank forms a continuous greenhouse or conservatory, being glazed both at its outer and inner edges with ordinary barn sash. A counter-high continuous seed and planter bed is thus formed which may be used for winter greens growing, for early seed flat forcing or flower raising and similar purposes. Every other sash is openable so that the plants may be easily attended to. Direct sunlight through the band of south windows plus stored warmth from the heat bank beneath are expected to maintain this mini-greenhouse at growing temperatures throughout the winter. Water outlets will be provided for convenient care of the plants. The section of south facade immediately facing the sunlit kitchen will differ somewhat from this design, in that the upper portion will be designed as a vegetable and fruit drier rather than as a conservatory. Thus the householders may prepare and dry a wide variety of foods conveniently from within the kitchen with far less time and greater convenience than traditional methods of direct exposure on shed roof or similar improvisations.

The house plan itself is fairly conventional (Figure C16) with a living room at the east end entered through a vestibule or airlock and with a generous corner fireplace in the northwest corner. The south end of this living room, directly adjacent to the glazed conservatory, serves as a dining area which is conveniently accessible via a pass-through opening from the kitchen.

A northside corridor serves a central bathroom and two bedrooms at the western end of the house. Opening off the north side of this corridor there are: a workshop, a cool-storage chamber and a combination laundry-rough food preparation room. These utility rooms need not be as well-heated as the rest and serve as buffers against the northern chill. There is also *portal* space for the sheltered storage of firewood here.

The main supplementary heat source is a small wood burning furnace located in its own compartment central to the house and convenient to the wood storage portal. Warm air from this furnace is conducted by overhead ducts to the two bedrooms and living room, while subfloor cool air ducts draw cool air back to the furnace room for reheating. A low-wattage fan in this duct may be necessary to speed up circulation in unusually cold weather.

Immediately above this furnace room is a dormer or turret within which is housed the large well-insulated hot water tank for the house (**Figure C17**). This tank is heated primarily in the summertime by a solar panel embedded in the slope of the roof immediately south of the dormer. The tank is also heated by a heat exchanger in the chimney flue of the wood burning furnace below it, thus providing two sources of hot water for the house. The hot water tank is quite close to both kitchen and bathroom, thus eliminating a long supply run to these main points of use.

In installing the flue-pipe heat exchanger provision should be made for automatically bypassing it when the tank water reaches about 165° F. This is necessary to prevent boiling of the water during long periods of heater firing. This bypassing may be accomplished by a thermostatically controlled damper which diverts the flue gases into a bypass flue or a separate chimney.

The kitchen is a fairly conventional design except for the solar crop drier which forms the south exposure. (This drier may also be used for growing herbs during the winter months.) The kitchen is equipped with a wood burning range as well as a small LP gas stove for use in the summer, and with a conventional refrigerator. However, auxiliary cool storage is provided by the cool-storage chamber next to the laundry-food preparation room. This chamber is a modern equivalent of the traditional *subterraneo* or root cellar and is kept cool by massive walls, good insulation and a night sky radiating panel which maintains a reservoir of chilled brine to hold temperatures down within the chamber.

Traditional small corner fireplaces are provided in the two bedrooms and one larger one in the living room for esthetic reasons and for still another alternative source of warmth in extreme conditions.

The roof collector also serves as a summer cooling system by means of chimney-like vents placed at the high end which may be opened in the summertime. The hot air accumulated under the roof creates an updraft through these vents and sucks warm air from ceiling vents within the house itself, which are also opened during this period. Warm air is thus vented automatically from the house on hot sunny and still days and a gentle circulation created which tempers the house interior with no expenditure of energy.

It is to be noted that several features of this house are experimental—principally the novel use of the roof as a collector and the night sky cooling system. Hence it is not recommended as one of the tried designs suggested in this book. However, there is considerable evidence that the system has good potential.

The continuous southward sloping expanse of the roof will

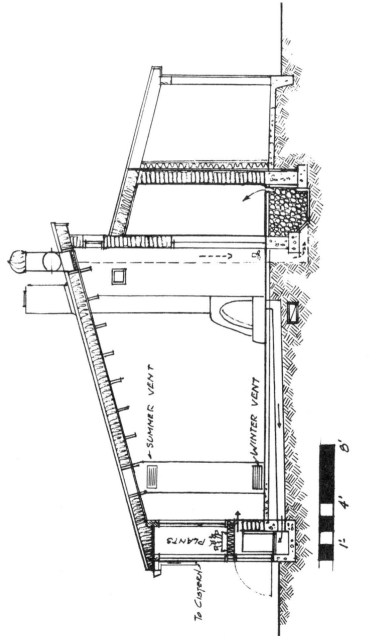

Fig. C 13

also be utilized as a rain and snow-melt collector by means of a gutter placed along the south edge with downspouts leading through filters to one or more underground cisterns. Water from these cisterns will probably be piped to the kitchen and utility rooms and raised by simple pitcher pumps to simplify

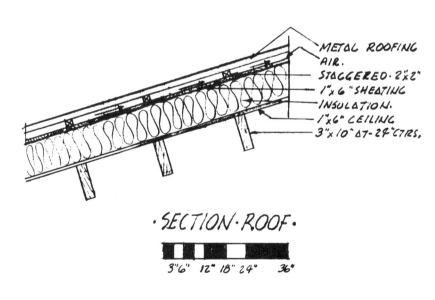

· SECTION · ROOF ·

3"6"   12" 18" 24"   36"

Fig. C 14

the installation as much as possible. This will supply soft water for special purposes and a generous reserve in case of power failure or breakdown of the water system.

A general view of the south facade of the house is shown in Figure C18.

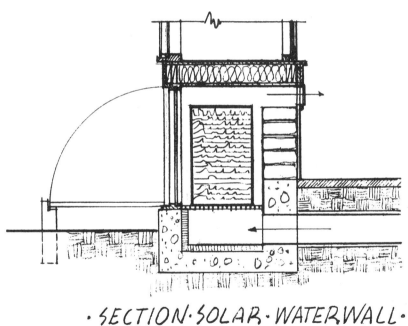

· SECTION · SOLAR · WATERWALL ·

3'6" 12" 18" 24"   36"

Fig. C 15

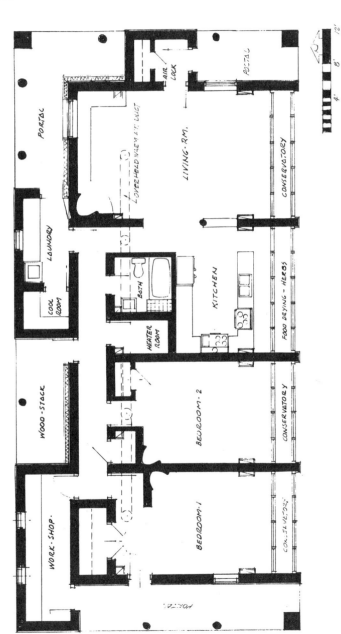

Fig. C16

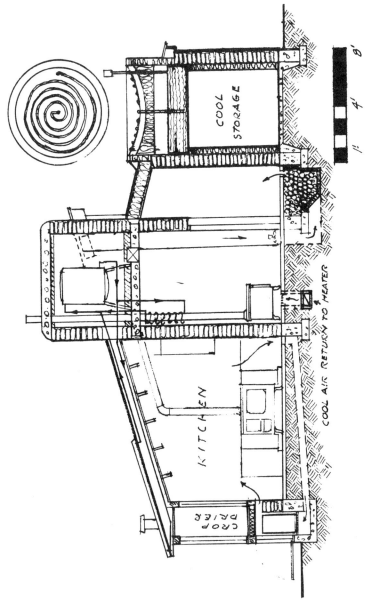

Fig. C 17

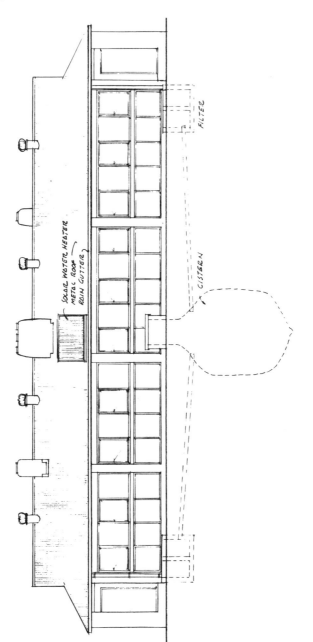

Fig. C 18

APPENDIX D

SOLAR CROP DRIERS

Several variations of solar vegetable and fruit driers developed in New Mexico are shown in the accompanying drawings. These all operate pretty much on the same principle: i.e., air heated in a small collector panel is conducted into the bottom of a drying chamber through which it rises by convection to exhaust vents at the top. Food to be dried is spread out on a series of mesh racks placed in the chamber so that the warmed air may pass freely around it. Glazed surfaces in the walls of the chamber also permit direct sunlight to strike the food, thus adding to the warming and drying effect. There may also be some sterilizing effect from the proportion of ultraviolet radiation which penetrates the glazing.

The following text was prepared by B. T. Rogers to describe the operation of the drier he has built and tested (Design No. D1), but in general it applies to the other units depicted. More complete descriptions of the latter may be obtained in a pamphlet published by the New Mexico Solar Energy Association, *How to Build a Solar Crop Dryer*, 50¢ (Design No. D3), and from the Brace Research Institute publication. *A Survey of Solar Agricultural Dryers*, McGill University, Ste. Anne de Bellevue, Quebec, Canada, $8.00. This publication contains many other examples from around the world. Four pages describing Design No. D2 may be obtained from the New Mexico Solar Energy Association, Box 2004, Santa Fe, N.M. 87501, 30¢ plus postage.

* * * * * *

The manner in which a crop drier operates is much more complicated than the casual observer might think. The serious worker in this area would do well to consult Chapter 9 of the *ASHRAE Handbook of Fundamentals* and Chapter 18 of the 1971 *Guide and Data Book* (also ASHRAE). The following description is highly truncated and simplified; it should be adequate for the small homesteader who wants to dry his produce.

When designing a drier for large quantities of a specific product, one must know a great deal about the rate at which moisture diffuses from the interior of the product to the surface where it can be carried away by the air. For the homesteader's application one must use the shotgun approach and try to design a drier that will work pretty well for a wide variety of produce but will not represent the best solution for any specific crop. My drier is expected to dry onion chips, walnuts, apricots, apples, mint, and most anything else that comes along, including laundry.

In simple terms, here is how my solar drier works:

1. Air flows by natural convection through a solar collector that heats the air. The collector has air flow on both sides of the blackened receptor. It has generous flow channels so the flow resistance is low and it moves a lot of air without too much temperature rise; it is a free-breathing collector. We must warm the air but it should not be allowed to get too hot. After all, we are trying to dry the produce, not cook it. During the full drying season the chamber temperature seldom rises above 120° F.

When air is heated the absolute humidity remains constant, but the relative humidity decreases and the air is hungry for moisture.

2. The moisture-hungry air now enters the drying chamber and is confronted with a mass of moist produce. A little thought at this point will reveal that our drier is now assuming the role of an evaporative cooler! As the air picks up moisture its temperature drops. This is where the energetics of solar drying come to the forefront: for each pound of moisture that we evaporate from the produce, we must supply about 1,000 B.T. U.s. The drier that we are considering has a rather unique feature. The drying chamber is also a solar collector. It is glazed on three sides. As the air is being cooled by evaporation it also is being heated by the sun. (An engineer would say that the process rises above the wet bulb line and thus increases the moisture burden.)

3. We now get rid of the air and throw it away along with the moisture that it has picked up. On a calm day the air flows out through the vent at the top of the drying chamber. Instead of a flue cap we have a small wind turbine at the top of the vent. We will say more about this later. This air is warmer than the ambient air (less dense) which encourages it to rise and it is also less dense because of its moisture burden. Moist air is lighter than dry air at the same temperature.

Some drier builders have tried to recirculate the air with the idea they are saving energy or something. They are wasting energy (their own) as the air humidity quickly comes to equilibrium—their drier becomes a low temperature steam cooker!

4. This drier operates by natural convection. The forces that produce natural convection are very delicate and easily overcome by wind gusts or a steady wind from an unfavorable direction. The wind turbine takes over under these circumstances and maintains flow through the drying chamber. A typical response to an unfavorable wind is for the chamber temperature to drop about 10° F., say, from 120° F. to 110° F. The flow of course increases to compensate for this temperature change and the drying process continues. Wind turbines are an

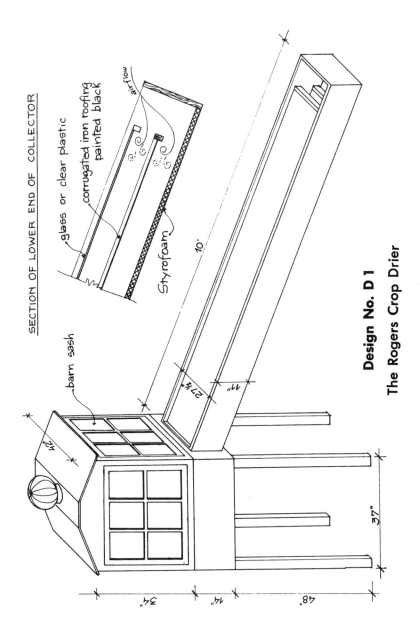

SECTION OF LOWER END OF COLLECTOR

glass or clear plastic

corrugated iron roofing
painted black

airflow

Styrofoam

barn sash

42"

27½"

11"

37"

10'

34"

14"

48"

Design No. D 1
The Rogers Crop Drier

inexpensive solution to all sorts of problems with naturally convective systems.

One of the nice things about this type of drier is that it tends to defeat many pests that plague the homesteader. By properly screening the flow passages and careful operation during the loading phase, you can avoid producing *high protein* dried fruit, i.e., a product infested with insect grubs. Another advantage involves walnuts. Walnuts are easily dried in the open without pest trouble, but you can lose a third of your crop

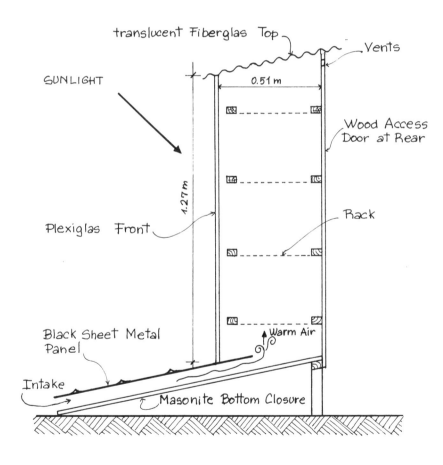

Design No. D 2 The van Dresser Drier

to piñon jays who are brave, crafty, fast and disrespectful. The drier does the job quickly and defeats the birds.

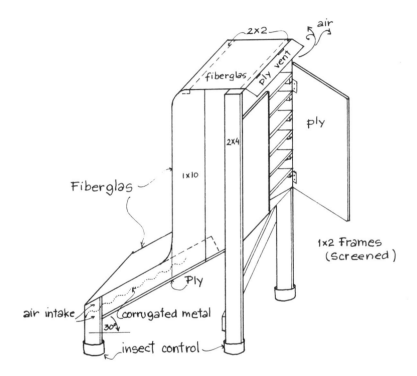

Design No. D 3   The Hopman Crop Drier

Ed. Note: Driers of this type also eliminate the need for rushing food racks under shelter whenever a rain shower comes up, as is necessary with customary open-air drying. They may also be built into the south wall of a kitchen so that fruits and vegetables prepared in the kitchen may be loaded into them directly without going outside. A number of versions of Designs D2 and D3 have been built around the State and operate successfully without turbine exhausts, but if a more positive air flow is needed turbine vents can be installed on their roofs as in the Rogers' design. In general, driers of this type will cut drying time to a quarter or a third required for open-air drying. They are not recommended for warm humid climates.

APPENDIX E

THE GHOST RANCH SOLAR DEMONSTRATION
AND TRAINING BUILDINGS

An offshoot of the Sundwellings Program was the Solar Housing Demonstration and Training Program funded jointly by the New Mexico Office of Manpower Administration, the Four Corners Regional Commission and the Ghost Ranch Conference Center. The objects of this program were threefold: to teach local builders and artisans the principles of simple climatically adapted construction using low-cost, low-energy native materials; to actually construct several prototypes of such buildings and make them available for continuous public inspection and demonstration; and to compare the thermal performance of several such buildings using differing (but all passive) systems of solar energy utilization.

To carry out these purposes, four simple two-bedroom dormitory cottages were designed by the Sundwellings team. Each building was 20' x 40', and of the same geometry except for the different solar absorption elements on the south facades. Three such elements were selected for trial: viz., a direct gain unit (large double-glazed windows, Figure E1); a Trombe wall unit (a dark wall of adobe behind double-glazing, vented at top and bottom to allow circulation of warmed air into the house, Figure E2); and a greenhouse unit (Figure E3). A control building was also constructed of the same dimensions and materials but with no special solar features other than ordinary windows in the south facade (Figure E4).

Locally available materials were used as largely as possible in these buildings—adobe brick made on the site, *vigas* or round ceiling beams cut in the adjoining forest, rough-sawn local lumber, flagstone quarried nearby, coarse sawdust for ceiling insulation and locally mined pumice for wall and perimeter insulation. The general style was derivative from the traditional folk architecture of the Hispanic Southwest. The construction was carried out by trainees from the region; some of them were Santa Clara and Jicarilla Apache Indian youths working under CETA auspices (Comprehensive Employment Training Act).

As this book goes to press, the four buildings are substantially complete and testing by physicists from the Los Alamos Scientific Laboratories (Solar Division) is beginning. During construction about 50 thermocouples were embedded at strategic points in each building—under the floors, in the walls, in the ceiling insulation, etc. Also a small weather station, including vertical and horizontal pyranometers, anemometer and ambient temperature gauge were installed. Readings from these sensors are being recorded and will be analyzed intensively at the end of the heating season.

In spite of the incompleteness of the buildings (not all have storm sash, night curtains, etc.), preliminary indications are that they will provide about 65 to 70% of their heating requirements from solar input. Additionally, the convection venting system (shown in Figure E5) performed well in the summer of 1976 and kept temperatures in the building at less than 75° F. when the outside temperature reached 95° F. Finally, thermosyphon solar water heaters, using antifreeze solution in the collector panels and jackets around the 40 gallon roof-mounted tanks for heat transfer, were designed and are partially completed. Figure E6 diagrams the logic of these installations.

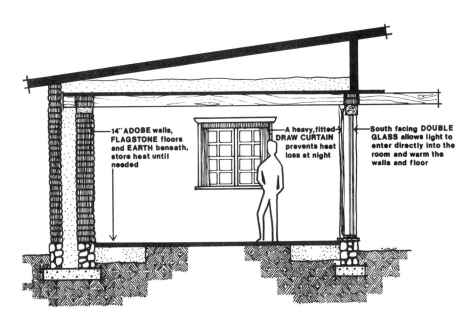

Fig. E 1   Direct Gain

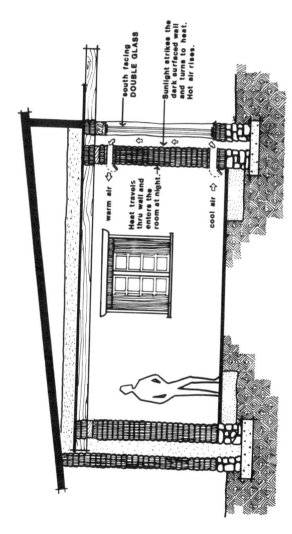

Fig. E 2 Trombe Wall

south facing DOUBLE GLASS

Sunlight strikes the dark surfaced wall and turns to heat. Hot air rises.

warm air

Heat travels thru wall and enters the room at night.

cool air

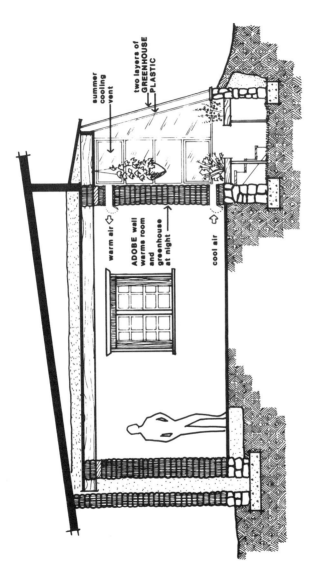

Fig. E 3   Greenhouse

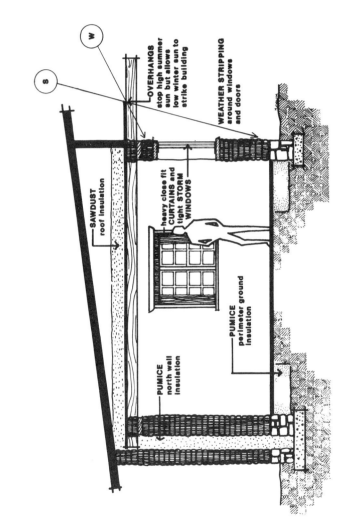

Fig. E 4 Control

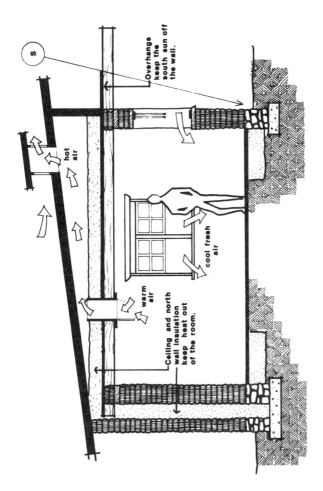

Fig. E 5   Summer Comfort

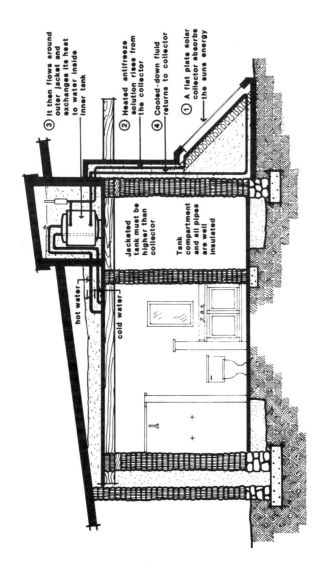

③ It then flows around outer jacket and exchanges its heat to water inside inner tank

② Heated antifreeze solution rises from the collector

④ Cooled-down fluid returns to collector

① A flat plate solar collector absorbs the suns energy

Jacketed tank must be higher than collector

Tank compartment and all pipes are well insulated

hot water

cold water

Fig. E 6 Water Heating

APPENDIX F

SOLAR ENERGY GLOSSARY

The following is adapted from glossaries prepared by: The Glossary Committee of the Taos Solar Energy Association; *Sun Earth*, by Richard Crowther, AIA, *et al.; Energy Primer*, published by Portola Institute; and the New Mexico Solar Energy Association.

Absorber plate or panel—a collector component that soaks up radiant energy from the sun. The heat is usually carried off by a circulating fluid such as water or air.

Absorbtivity—the ratio of absorbed to incident solar radiation. For the visible range, dark colors absorb light rays more readily than light colors; matte surfaces absorb better than shiny surfaces. Used here in reference to solar absorber panels and/or their finishes. Measured as the amount of radiation absorbed as a percentage of incident radiation available.

Active system—requires importation of energy from outside the immediate environment: e.g., energy to operate fans and pumps.

Air change—the replacement of a quantity of air in a volume within a given period of time.

Air mass—the volume of atmosphere through which the sun's rays travel to reach the earth's surface. When the sun is directly overhead, this volume and, consequently, the distance traveled through it, is at its lowest value. This is sometimes called "air mass 1." At ten degrees above the horizon, sunlight is passing through approximately seven times as much atmosphere (air mass) as at air mass 1.

Altitude—see solar altitude.

Ambient temperature—surrounding temperature, as temperature around a house.

Auxiliary system (furnace)—a supplementary heating unit to provide heat to a space when its primary (in this context solar) unit cannot do so.

Azimuth—the horizontal angle formed between two lines: one from an observation point to a cardinal reference direction, such as north or south; the other from the observation point to an object such as the sun.

Back-up system—see auxiliary system.

Berm—earth mounded, as alongside a ditch. In solar construction usage, earth mounded against a house wall or over a roof.

Bioconversion (*biofuels*)—conversion of solar energy to fuel by natural methods (such as fermentation or decomposition) from organic materials, as manure or plant wastes.

Biosphere—the zone of air, land, water at the earth's surface, occupied by plants and animals.

Calorie—a unit of heat (metric measure). The amount of energy equivalent to that needed to raise the temperature of one gram of water one degree Centigrade. One "large" or "kilogram calorie" (1,000 small calories) is approximately equal to 4 B.T.U.s.

Change of state—see latent heat.

Collector—a device for capturing solar energy, ranging from ordinary windows to complex focusing optical concentrators.

Collector angle (collector tilt)—the angle between the surface of a flat collector and the horizontal plane. A collector surface receives the greatest possible amount of sunshine when its orientation is perpendicular to the sun's rays.

Concentrator—a device used to intensify solar radiation.

Conduction—the transfer of heat through materials (solids, liquids or gases) by molecular excitation of adjacent molecules.

Convection—the circulation of gases or liquids. In natural convection the movement occurs as a result of the tendency of hot fluids to be less dense and rise and cold fluids to be more dense and sink. In forced convection the fluids are moved by a device such as a fan.

Cost-effective—worth the money. A system is cost-effective when the long-term savings are greater than the long-term costs.

Dead air space—a confined space of air. A dead air space tends to reduce both conduction and convection of heat. This fact is utilized in virtually all insulating materials and systems, such as double glazing, Fiberglas bats, rigid foam panels, fur and hair, and loose-fill insulation such as pumice, vermiculite, rock wool, styrofoam beads and goose down.

Degree day (for cooling)—see degree day for heating, except that the base temperature is established at 70° F., and cooling degree days are measured above that base.

Degree day (for heating)—an expression of a climatic heating requirement expressed by the difference in degrees F. below the average outdoor temperature for each day and an established base of 65° F. (The assumption behind selecting this base is that average construction will provide interior comfort with no artificial heat input when the exterior temperature is 65° F.)

delta T—a difference in temperature (sometimes written Δt).

Diffuse radiation—sunlight diffused by air molecules or reflected from particles in the atmosphere, such as dust or moisture. It comes from all directions, not in parallel beams.

Direct gain—solar energy collected (as heat) in a building without special solar collection devices. Examples: through windows or absorbed by roof and outside walls.

Double glazing—a sandwich of two separated layers of glass or transparent plastic enclosing air to create an insulating barrier.

Dry bulb temperature—a measure of the sensible temperature of air (the one with which we are most familiar).

Duct—a channel or tube through which air or other gases flow.

Efficiency, thermal—the ratio of the useful heat produced at the point of use in a given time period to the thermal energy input during the same time period, expressed as per cent.

Emissivity—the property of emitting heat radiation; possessed by all materials to a varying extent. "Emittance" is the numerical value of this property, expressed as a decimal fraction, for a particular material. Normal emittance is the value measured at 90 degrees to the plane of the sample, and hemispherical emittance is the total amount emitted in all directions. We are generally interested in hemispherical, rather than normal, emittance. Emittance values range from 0.05 for brightly polished metals to 0.96 for flat black paint. Most non-metals have high values of emittance.

Energy—the capacity for doing work; taking a number of forms which may be transformed from one into another, such as thermal (heat), mechanical (work), electrical, and chemical. It is most generally measured in kilowatt hours or British Thermal Units.

Energy storage—the ability to fix energy by conversion to other forms (thermal, kinetic, potential, chemical, etc.) for later retrieval for useful purposes.

Eutectic salts—salts used for storing heat. At a given temperature salts melt, absorbing large amounts of heat which will be released as the salts freeze. Example: Glauber's salts. The melt-freeze temperatures vary with different salts and some occur at convenient temperatures for thermal storage such as in the range of 80° to 120° F.

Flat plate collector—an assembly containing a panel of metal or other suitable material, usually a flat black color on its sun side, that absorbs sunlight and converts it into heat. This panel is usually in an insulated box, glazed with glass or plastic on the sun side to retard heat loss. In the collector this heat transfers to a circulating liquid or gas, such as air, water, oil, antifreeze or paraffin, which carries it for use elsewhere.

Flow rate—velocity at which a fluid travels, usually through an opening or duct.

Fresnel lens—a focusing lens, similar to a magnifying glass except that the focusing is achieved at lower cost by a series of concentric or parallel forms engraved or molded on a flat surface of glass or plastic.

Frostline—the depth of frost penetration in the earth. This depth varies from one geographic location to another.

Glazing—a covering of transparent or translucent material (glass or plastic) for admitting light. Glazing retards heat losses from reradiation and convection. Examples: windows, skylights, greenhouses and collector coverings.

Greenhouse effect—refers to the characteristic tendency of some transparent materials such as glass to transmit radiation shorter than about 2.5 microns and block radiation of longer wavelengths ("heat rays").

Heat exchanger—a device for transferring heat from one fluid medium to another such as the old-fashioned heating radiator (water to air), a gas water heater (hot gas to water) or a solar water heater (air or antifreeze to water). Heat exchangers always require a temperature gradient between the two media and therefore lose heat in the exchange process.

Heat gain—an increase in the amount of heat contained in a space, resulting from direct solar radiation and the heat given off by people, lights, equipment, machinery and other sources.

Heat loss—a decrease in the amount of heat contained in a space, resulting from heat flow through walls, windows, roofs and other building envelope components.

Heat pipe—a closed pipe containing a refrigerant, wick and air space which will rapidly transfer heat from one end to the other without any input of work.

Heat pump—a device which transfers thermal energy or heat from a relatively low-temperature reservoir to one at a higher temperature. Heat normally flows from a warmer region to a cooler region; this process is reversed when additional energy is supplied by a heat pump.

Heat sink—a body which is capable of accepting and storing heat and, therefore, may also act as a heat source.

Heliostat—an instrument consisting of a mirror mounted on an axis rotated by clockwork or other mechanism, used to steadily reflect the sun in one direction.

Heliotropism—tendency to face towards the sun or other light source.

Horsepower—a unit of power equaling 2,544 B.T.U.s per hour, 550 foot-pounds per second or 746 watts per hour.

Incident angle—the angle between the sun's rays and a line perpendicular (normal) to the irradiated surface.

Infiltration—the uncontrolled loss or gain of heat from air leaks through cracks in a building wall. It works either way: cold air leaking in during cold weather; the reverse in hot weather.

Insolation—incident solar radiation: the solar radiation received per unit area of surface. Insolation is usually measured in Langleys (see below) or B.T.U.s per square foot per hour or per day.

Insulation—materials or systems used to prevent loss or gain of heat, usually employing very small dead air spaces to limit conduction and/or convection.

Kilowatt—a unit of electric power equal to 1,000 watts.

Laminar air flow—the smooth movement of layered air, usually the optimum condition in a duct system for air transport. It is not desirable at heat exchanger surfaces where turbulent flow is necessary.

Langley—the meteorologist's unit of solar radiation intensity, equivalent to 1.0 gram calorie per square centimeter, usually used in terms of Langleys per minute. 1 Langley per minute = 221.2 B.T.U.s per hour per square foot.

Latent heat—heat content of a substance which is not indicated by its "sensible" temperature but is embodied in the internal molecular state of the substance (e.g., whether it is liquid or frozen). Heat energy stored in liquid water, for example, may be liberated when it freezes without change of temperature.

Latitude—the angular distance north (+) or south (—) of the equator, measured in degrees of arc.

Passive system—operates on the natural energy available in the immediate environment.

Photolysis—chemical decomposition caused by the action of

radiant energy.

Photosynthesis—the process in which the sun's radiation, in certain specific wavelengths, causes water, carbon dioxide and nutrients to react, thus producing oxygen and carbohydrates in plants.

Plenum—a chamber in an air-handling system for equalizing air flow.

Power—the rate at which work is performed or energy expended.

Pyranometer—a solar radiometer which measures total insolation, including both the direct and the diffuse radiation.

Quad—10^{15} B.T.U.s (one quadrillion B.T.U.s).

Radiation—one of the three ways heat is transferred (the others are conduction and convection). Radiation is the direct transport of energy through space, needing no air or other medium for its transmission.

Reflectance—the ratio of the amount of light reflected by a surface to the amount absorbed. Good light reflectors are not necessarily good heat reflectors.

Refraction—the change in direction of light rays as they enter a transparent medium such as water, air or glass. Rays bend more the farther from the perpendicular the light hits, the greater the density or the longer the wavelength.

Retrofitting—attaching systems or equipment to existing structures, as in the case of a roof-mounted water heater or an add-on greenhouse.

r factor—a unit of thermal resistance used for comparing insulating values of different materials; the reciprocal of the conductivity.

Selective surface—a surface that has a high absorptance of incoming solar radiation but low emittance of longer wavelengths (heat).

Sensible heat—heat that results in a temperature change.

Solar altitude—an angle, measured in a vertical plane, from a point of reference on the earth's surface, one leg of which is horizontal, the other leg of which is pointing at the sun.

Solar cell—also photovoltaic cell. A device employing semiconductors, which when exposed to solar radiation, generates an electric current.

Solar constant—429 B.T.U.s per square foot per hour at equinox, the maximum amount of solar radiation that passes through extra-atmospheric space at a given earth-sun distance. In the Northern Hemisphere, the solar constant is

7% greater in winter than summer.

Space heating—interior heating of a building or room.

Specific heat—the heat capacity of a substance per unit of weight. The specific heat of water is 1 B.T.U. per pound; the specific heat of rock is .22 B.T.U. per pound. The higher the specific heat of a substance, the greater its heat-storage capacity.

Sunshine—the total radiation from the sun inside the atmosphere.

Suntempered—direct use of the sun's energy to heat a space without resorting to a powered system for collection and storage.

Sun-time—time of day as determined by the position of the sun.

Temperature gradient—the profile of temperature change within an assembly.

Therm—100,000 B.T.U.s.

Thermal conductance—the amount of heat in B.T.U.s which can be conducted through a particular solid material, one foot square, which is 1 inch thick and has a temperature difference of 1° F. maintained between its two surfaces. "k" is the symbol used here to designate thermal conductance. Most metals are good conductors and their conductivity varies with their temperature. At 212° F. (100° C.), silver transmits 2,856 B.T.U.s/°F./in., while mild steel transmits only 311 B.T.U.s/°F./in.

Thermal mass—the amount of potential heat storage capacity available in a given assembly or system. Waterwalls, concrete floors and adobe walls are examples of thermal mass.

Thermal resistance—the reciprocal of thermal conductance. The thermal resistance of a material is its thickness, l, in inches divided by its thermal conductivity, k. The resistance of a series of different materials, all in thermal contact with each other, is the sum of the individual resistances.

Thermal storage—thermal capacity of a mass to store heat as a function of a given temperature change.

Thermocouple—a thermoelectric device which has a combination of two dissimilar wires with their ends connected together. A millivolt meter is connected in the circuit to measure the voltage which is generated when the two junctions are at different temperatures. If one junction is kept in a bath of ice and water, at 32° F., the voltage generated (measured in millivolts) is a measure of the temperature of the other junction above 32° F. reference point.

Thermosyphon—the convective circulation of fluid which occurs in a closed system when less-dense warm fluid rises, displaced by denser, cooler fluid in the same system.

Tracking—the daily following of the sun by a collector assembly, used to increase collection efficiency and/or collection temperature. Usually required for focusing systems.

Transmittance—the ratio of radiant energy transmitted through a transparent surface to energy incident on it. In solar technology, it is often affected by the thickness and composition of the glass cover plates on a collector, and to a major extent by the angle of incidence between the sun's rays and a line normal to the surface.

U factor (U value)—a coefficient which indicates the energy (B.T.U.) conducted through a substance for every degree (Fahrenheit) of temperature difference from one side to the other under steady state conditions. The reciprocal of the resistance (r) factor.

Vapor barrier—a component of construction, usually a membrane, which is impervious to the flow of moisture and air.

Waterwall—an interior wall of water-filled containers constituting a one-step heating system which combines collection and storage.

Watt—a unit of electrical power. Watts = volts × amperes; 1,000 watts = 1 kilowatt; 1 kilowatt-hour = 3,413 B.T.U.s.

Wet bulb temperature—the lowest temperature attainable by evaporating water into the air without altering the energy content.

Work—the expenditure of energy measured by multiplying a force by the displacement of its point of application along its line of action.

APPENDIX G

INTERIM REPORT

Thermal Performance of the Ghost Ranch
*Sundwellings Solar Test Cottages**

As indicated in Appendix E, monitoring of these buildings was carried out by instrumentation installed and supervised by the Solar Division of Los Alamos Scientific Laboratory. At this writing, the Laboratory has not released an official report on the results of this monitoring, but sufficient data has been made available so that several workers in the field have been able to make reasonably sound evaluations.

The most useful data was collected during the month of February, 1978, when the buildings were evacuated and pilot lights in the butane auxiliary heaters were turned off. Figure

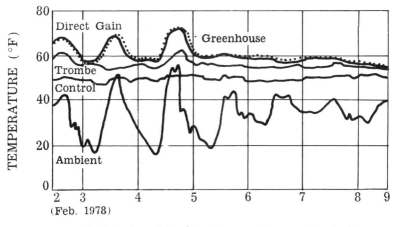

(Ambient and Inside Temperatures—Facsimile
of LASL Computer Plot)

Fig. G 1

G 1 is a facsimile of the recorder plot for one week in February, and Figure G 2, prepared by Mark Chalom, summarizes the results numerically. Figure G 3 illustrates the intensity of the solar radiation falling on the south walls during this period, in BTUs per square foot.

(BUILDING PERFORMANCE)

Building	Avg. Mean	Avg. Daily Mean Low	Avg. Daily High
Control	44.8°	43.7°	46.5°
Trombe	54.2°	52.3°	56.9°
Direct Gain	57.3°	52.5°	64.6°
Greenhouse	58.6°	54.9°	65.6°
Outside Ambient	32.2°	20.7°	46.7°

Fig. G 2

(MONTHLY SOLAR INSOLATION—67% Possible)

BTUs per square foot per day measured on south vertical wall

Lowest = 361 BTU/□/D
Highest = 1939 BTU/□/D
Average = 1300 BTU/□/D

Fig. G 3

To translate these figures into approximations of the efficiency, or more properly, the percentage of solar contribution to each building's heating load, B. T. Rogers made the following assumptions: (a) an internal temperature of 65°F would constitute full heating for an unoccupied building with no internal heat source; (b) the difference between the mean temperature (about 30°) for February at this location and the desired 65°F internal temperature, or 65−30 = 35°, would measure the necessary heating contribution; and (c) the difference between the measured mean internal temperature and the mean external temperature, as a percentage of 35°, would represent the solar contribution.

On this basis the four buildings were rated as follows:

$$\text{Control} \quad \frac{10}{35} \quad = \quad 28\%$$

$$\text{Trombe} \quad \frac{20}{35} \quad = \quad 57\%$$

$$\text{Direct Gain} \quad \frac{24}{35} \quad = \quad 68\%$$

$$\text{Greenhouse} \quad \frac{27}{35} \quad = \quad 77\%$$

Figure G 4, prepared by Quentin Wilson, presents the data

for the month in a different format, including such information as the ratio of glazing to floor area, and range of interior temperature variations. This table indicates a somewhat closer matching of the performances of the Direct Gain and Greenhouse units. Wilson concludes that the Greenhouse unit has only a "slight edge" over the Direct Gain. The discrepancy may be due to the fact that Rogers used data from a single charac-

(TABULATED PERFORMANCE DATA)

	Control	Trombe	Dir. Gn.	Grnhs.
Floor Area	566'²	566'²	588'²	574'²
Glazing Area	19'²	148'²	134'²	217'²
Glazing/Floor Ratio	.03	.26	.23	.38
Inside Temp. Range	4°F	6°F	17°F	17°F
Outside Temp. Range	38°F	38°F	38°F	38°F
Range Ratio	.11	.16	.45	.45
Inside Temp. Average	48°F	54°F	65°F	65°F
Outside Temp. Avg.	32°F	32°F	32°F	32°F
Avg. Temp. Difference	16°F	22°F	33°F	33°F

Fig. G 4

teristic February day, rather than the average for the month.

In any case the general performance is close to, or slightly better than, the 65-70% estimated in advance by the designers.

The relatively poor performance of the Trombe Wall unit should not be taken as indication of proof of the inferior efficiency of that system. The mullions used in the glazing were unnecessarily massive (2"x6") and caused considerable shading, especially in mid-morning and mid-afternoon. Wilson estimates the percentage of shading at 34% for noon plus or minus two hours on December 21. Performance would be considerably improved if the mullions were narrower and the glazing placed at their outer surfaces. Rogers also suggests that the shortness of these walls might also decrease the effectiveness of their performance, as the ratio of heat-losing end surfaces to heat-collecting south exposures is relatively high.

Well-fitting external insulating shutters on the Trombe Wall would improve the performance of this building, and of the Direct Gain building as well.

The not negligible solar performance of the Control Unit came somewhat as a surprise. It should be noted in this connection that this building, though not equipped with any special solar aperture, nevertheless had the double insulated north wall and a solar oriented south facade, which acted as an unglazed Trombe wall. Figure G 5 shows the temperature fluctuations of this wall at several points during three days in February. These curves illustrate the much-discussed thermal flywheel effect of adobe construction, by which strong exter-

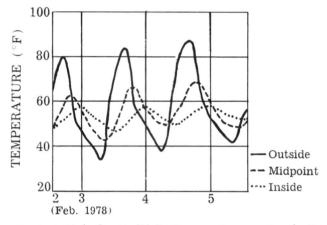

(Control Unit South Wall Temperatures—Facsimile of LASL Computer Plot)

Fig. G 5

nal diurnal fluctuations in temperature are smoothed out and retarded in phase, thus tending to stabilize conditions within the structure. This building and the Trombe Wall building performed best in terms of minimizing internal temperature variations (4° and 6° respectively) while the Direct Gain and Greenhouse fluctuated about 17°.

There was some dissatisfaction with the relative dimness of the interior of the Trombe cottage, due to the absence of any see-through south windows. This could of course be remedied by piercing the Trombe wall with appropriate openings.

The convective solar water heaters performed satisfactorily, but their output had to be used frugally, as the storage tanks are only of about 40 gallon capacity and there is no booster auxiliary.

*Grateful acknowledgement is made to Mark Chalom, B. T. Rogers and Quentin Wilson. Some of the material and data in this Interim Report has been abstracted from papers and evaluations prepared by them.

Bibliography

Building Techniques Appropriate to the Southwest:

Adobe News, all issues, Box 702, Los Lunas, N.M. 87031, $8 annually.

Cytryn, S., *Soil Construction*, Weizman Science Press of Israel, Jerusalem, 183 pp., 1957.

Lumpkins, W., *Adobe Past and Present*, Museum of N.M., Santa Fe, $1.95, 39 pp., 1974.

McHenry, P., *Adobe Build-It-Yourself*, University of Arizona Press, Tucson, $7.95, 157 pp., 1976.

Steadman, M., *Adobe Architecture*, Sunstone Press, Santa Fe, $3.95, 48 pp., 1975.

U. S. Department of Housing and Urban Development, Office of International Affairs, *Handbook for Building Homes of Earth*, Washington, D. C., 159 pp., n.d.

Food Storage:

Batchelor, W. D., *Gateway to Survival is Food Storage*, Box 15711, Salt Lake City, $2.00, 105 pp., 1974.

Loveday, E., *Home Storage of Fruits and Vegetables*, Garden Way Publ., Charlotte, Vt., 160 pp., n.d.

Robinson, C., *Plans for a Harvest Kitchen*, Garden Way Publ., Charlotte, Vt., $2.50, 40 pp., n.d.

U. S. Department of Agriculture, *Home Storage of Vegetables and Fruits*, Bulletin No. 1934, 10¢, 29 pp., 1943.

Greenhouse Design and Management:

Blake, C., *Greenhouse Gardening for Fun*, Garden Way Publ., Charlotte, Vt., $2.45, 256 pp., n.d.

DeKorne, J. B., *The Survival Greenhouse*, Walden Foundation, Box 5, El Rito, N.M. 87530, $7.50, 165 pp., 1975.

132

Encyclopaedia Britannica, 11th ed., "Horticulture," pp. 741-783, 1911.

Fisher, R., and Yanda, B., *The Food and Heat Producing Solar Greenhouse*, John Muir Publications, Box 613, Santa Fe, $6.00, 161 pp., 1976.

Yanda, W. and S., *An Attached Solar Greenhouse*, in English and Spanish, The Lightning Tree, Santa Fe, $2.00, 18 pp., 1976.

Siting, Landscaping, Gardening, Small Animal Husbandry:

Adams, A., *Your Energy Efficient House*, Garden Way Publ., Charlotte, Vt., $4.85, n.d.

Crowther, R. I., *Sun Earth*, Crowther and Solar Group Architects, 810 Steele St., Denver, Colo., $13.95, 232 pp., 1976.

Jeavons, J., "How to Grow More Vegetables," *Ecology Action of the Midpeninsula*, 555 Santa Cruz Ave., Menlo Park, Ca., 82 pp., n.d.

Kern, K., *The Owner Built Homestead*, Oakhurst, Ca., $5.00, 209 pp., 1974.

Robinson, E. and C., *The Have-More Plan*, Garden Way Publ., Charlotte, Vt., $2.50, 70 pp., n.d.

Solar Heating Technology, General:

Anderson, B., *Solar Energy and Shelter Design*, Total Environmental Action, Church Hill, Harrisville, N.H., $7.00, 1973.

Anderson, B., with Riordan, M., *The Solar Home Book*, Cheshire Books, Harrisville, N.H., $7.50, 297 pp., 1976.

Balcomb, J. D., and Keller, M., editors, *Passive Solar Heating and Cooling Conference and Workshop Proceedings*, (May 18-19, 1976), LASL, Solar Energy Group Q-11, Mail Stop 571, Los Alamos, N.M., Los Alamos Scientific Laboratories Report No. LA 6637C, 355 pp., 1977.

Branley, F. M., *Solar Energy*, Crowell Co., N.Y., $3.95, 1957.

Daniels, F., *Direct Use of the Sun's Energy*, Ballantine Books, N.Y., $1.95, 271 pp., 1975.

Los Alamos Scientific Laboratories, *Solar Heating Handbook for Los Alamos*, Report No. LA 5967, Los Alamos, N.M., $4.00, 72 pp., 1975.

New Mexico Solar Energy Association, *Third Annual Life-Technics Conference, Ghost Ranch Conference Center*, (Oct. 12-13, 1974), Santa Fe, $6.00, 187 pp.

Shurcliff, W. A., *Solar Heated Buildings, A Brief Survey*, 13th and Final Edition, 19 Appleton St., Cambridge, Ma. 02138, $13.00, 306 pp., 1977.

U. S. Department of Urban Development, *Solar Energy and Your Home*, free pamphlet, 19 pp., 1976. Order from National Solar Heating and Cooling Information Center, Box 1607, Rockville, Md. 20850.

Williams, J. R., *Solar Energy Technology and Applications*, Box 14251, Ann Arbor, Mich., $6.95, 1974.

Yellott, J. I., *Solar Energy Utilization for Heating and Cooling*, American Section, International Solar Energy Society, Williams College, Williamstown, Ma., $1.00, 20 pp., 1974.

Solar Water Heaters and Driers:

Anon., *Hot Water*, Hot Water, 350 E. Mountain Dr., Santa Barbara, Ca., $2.00, n.d.

Brace Research Institute, McGill University, *How to Build a Solar Water Heater*, Ste. Anne de Bellevue, Quebec, Canada, $1.25, 1975.

_____, *How to Make a Solar Cabinet Drier for Agricultural Produce*, Ste. Anne de Bellevue, Quebec, Canada, $1.25, 1973.

E. I. & I. Associates, *Solar Energy Guide of Flat Plate Collectors for Home Application*, Box 37, Newburg Park, Ca., $2.00, n.d.

Florida Energy Committee, *How to Build a Solar Water Heater*, 985 Orange Ave., Winter Park, Fla., $3.30, 1976.

New Mexico Solar Energy Association, *How to Build a Solar Crop Dryer*, Santa Fe, 50¢, 8 pp., 1976.

Zomeworks Corp., *Solar Water Heater Plans*, Box 712, Albuquerque, N.M., $5.00, 1974.

Wood Heating:

Gay, L., *Heating with Wood*, Garden Way Publ., Charlotte, Vt., $3.00, 128 pp., n.d.

Havens, D., *The Woodburner's Handbook*, Wiscasset, Ma., $2.95, 96 pp., n.d.

Sanchez, L., "Building the Corner Fireplace," *Adobe News*, Los Lunas, N.M., pp. 3-5, with detailed illustrations, July-August 1975.

Shelton, J., *The Woodburner's Encyclopedia*, Wood Energy Institute, 5 So. State St., Concord, N.H., $6.95, 155 pp., 1976.

Steadman, M., *Adobe Fireplaces*, Sunstone Press, Santa Fe, $1.25, 10 pp., 1974.

Wood Burning Quarterly, 8009 34 Ave. So., Minneapolis, Minn., $4.95 annually.

Wood 'n Energy, quarterly journal of Wood Energy Institute, 5 So. State St., Concord, N.H., $15 with membership.

Index